TEAM INTERPRETING

AS COLLABORATION AND INTERDEPENDENCE

JACK HOZA

A publication of RID Press
A division of the Registry of Interpreters for the Deaf, Inc.
333 Commerce Street, Alexandria VA 22314

Registry of Interpreters for the Deaf, Inc.

RID Press is a division of the Registry of Interpreters for the Deaf, Inc.,
333 Commerce Street, Alexandria VA 22314, USA
703.838.0030 (V), 703.838.0459 (TTY), 703.838.0454 (Fax).

Published 2010

Internet:www.rid.org

ISBN 978-0-916883-52-2

Library of Congress Control Number: 2010920098

Printed in the United States of America

SUSTAINABLE
FORESTRY
INITIATIVE
Certified Fiber Sourcing
www.sfiprogram.org

TABLE OF CONTENTS

Interdependence is the paradigm of *we* – *we* can do it; *we* can cooperate; *we* can combine our talents and abilities and create something greater together.

—Stephen R. Covey, *The Seven Habits of Highly Effective People*

To interpreters who have an open mind and an open heart

PREFACE

This book is about how interpreters work together in teams. Much has been written about the process by which an interpreter determines equivalent meaning in the target language, and how interpreters manage their work and make important professional, ethical, and meaning-based decisions. Although team interpreting is commonplace in interpreting assignments that are lengthy, complex, or particularly challenging, little study has been made of this important feature of the interpreting profession. Teaming has the potential to enrich the interpretation, provide additional support for the interpreters, and enable participants in the interpreted interaction to better achieve their goals. This book represents the first major published volume that addresses team interpreting.

WHY I WROTE THIS BOOK

The idea for writing this book on team interpreting was slow in coming. As a professional interpreter and interpreter educator, I have had many years of experience with both team interpreting and introducing advanced interpreting students to teaming. Our field's understanding of team interpreting over the years has been based largely on anecdotal evidence. Interpreters tend to share with each other what they believe makes for a successful team, and they use this understanding to help mentor newer interpreters about teaming. Like other interpreters and interpreter educators, I have felt confident sharing my experience with teaming and the strategies that I believe work for team interpreting. In particular, I have shared my belief that a good relationship and a sense of openness between the team members are of utmost importance for a team to work successfully.

Nevertheless, we have all been working in somewhat of a vacuum, in that we have primarily been informed by our own experiences. This is a natural first step in the development of understanding something new. Our understanding of team interpreting is similar to how interpreting itself was understood in the early days of the profession. Although the field of American Sign Language (ASL)/English interpretation officially began in the middle of the 1960s, it took some twenty years before models of the interpreting process (such as those by Cokely, Colonomos, and Seleskovitch) emerged as leading models in the field.[1] Prior to that time, practitioners passed on what they believed to be the best way to approach the interpreting process. This is happening for the most part with team interpreting. Practitioners have their own ideas of what is needed for teaming, but my goal in writing this book is to use a more scientific approach to help bring to light what is involved in the process of team interpreting, what factors contribute to an effective team, and what still needs to be researched further.

Like many others, I have relied on similar resources to inform my understanding of team interpreting. These resources include depending on my own experience with teaming, discussing team interpreting with other interpreters, taking workshops on team interpreting, and reading materials primarily from the RID *VIEWS* and the *Journal of Interpretation*, both of which are publications of the Registry of Interpreters for the Deaf (RID). I was not satisfied with what was available on this topic, so I conducted a literature review, and I found that much of the literature covered the same few topics and rarely went beyond these topics.

Two articles, however, stood out from the rest for me personally, in terms of their contributions to the field. One is an essay titled "Beyond Correction and Critique: Working in Teams" by Tim Kinsella, which challenges the prevailing view of team interpreting and asks readers to be more forward-thinking in how teams accomplish their work together.[2] The other is an article titled "Interpreting in Teams: A Pilot Study on Requesting and Offering Support" by Dennis Cokely and Jennifer Hawkins, which reports on the detailed findings of a research study that investigated how teams of interpreters make requests for support and offers of support.[3] Cokely and Hawkins find that the cues interpreters actually use to request support in practice differ from what they believe they use. Both of these articles served as inspiration for me for two very different reasons. The first provided me with motivation to look beneath the surface of our work as teams, to the underlying philosophical issues and assumptions that are important for us to consider. The second provided me with a desire to further explore what interpreters actually do in their team interpreting work.[4]

As a result, I conducted two research studies in order to better understand team interpreting. The first study involved videotaping teams of interpreters interpreting the same material and interviewing the individual interpreters afterwards. I was pleased with what this study revealed about team interpreting. At the same time, I saw that a further study was warranted, so I conducted a national survey of certified interpreters. The survey allowed for a broader study of team interpreting and further elaborated important areas of teaming. These two studies form the basis for this book.

THOUGHT QUESTIONS

A series of THOUGHT QUESTIONS appears at the beginning of major sections of each chapter in the book, as well as at the end of each chapter. These questions are designed to help readers enhance their understanding of team interpreting and the teaming relationship. Readers can use the THOUGHT QUESTIONS to help explore particular topics before reading the relevant sections of a chapter and to assist in processing chapter topics at the conclusion of each chapter. Individuals can use the THOUGHT QUESTIONS for journal writing; interpreting classes or groups of interpreters can use the questions to stimulate discussion in the classroom, in a workshop, or online; and teams of interpreters can use them to process their own work and to apply the major points of each chapter. The questions assume some experience with team interpreting; however, students of interpretation who do not have this experience may rely on their observations of teams or interviews with interpreters.

TERMINOLOGY

The interpreters who participated in the two studies used terms that were sometimes imprecise or ambiguous. To assist the reader, we will now briefly review several such terms and define how they are used in the book.

First, as interpreters, we use several terms to refer to the people for whom we interpret. We may call them *consumers* or *clients* if we view our work from more of a service model; we may call them *participants, speakers (or signers)*, or *interlocutors* if we view our work from more of a theoretical framework; or we may call them *people* or may refer to them by their *roles* (such as doctor, employee, supervisor, or legislator) if we use more of a practical, descriptive model. In this book, we use *people* when discussing a collective group, such as *Deaf people* or *hearing people*, and we use *participants, speakers*, or *signers* when we talk about the primary participants in the interpreted interaction. In addition, the term *speakers* is sometimes used in a general sense to mean both English speakers and ASL signers.

Second, there are various terms used to describe the hearing status of the people with whom we work:

Deaf - a cultural identity; the community of those who use ASL,
deaf - an audiological term used to describe a severe to profound
　　degree of hearing loss,
hard of hearing - an audiological term used to describe a moderate to
　　mild degree of hearing loss,
hearing - a term used to describe those who are not D/deaf and who,
　　generally, are not part of Deaf culture, and
hearing impaired - a general term used by many hearing people to
　　refer to those who are D/deaf and hard of hearing.[5]

All of these terms not only have different meanings, they also have different connotations. For example, the term *Deaf* is highly valued by members of Deaf culture; the term *hearing impaired* is preferred by many hearing people, but is offensive to the majority of Deaf people; and the term *hearing* is commonly used in the literature, but most hearing people have never heard the term.

It is common in the field to refer to the people we work with as either *Deaf* or *hearing* (and, sometimes, *deaf* or *hearing*). In this book, we continue this practice and use the terms *Deaf* and *hearing* to refer to ASL signers (Deaf people) and English speakers (hearing people), respectively. Because the majority of the ASL-signing community is on its own particular journey to Deafhood (identity as a Deaf person), we refer to members of this community as *Deaf* and avoid the labels *deaf* and *hard of hearing*.[6] In fact, many of those in this community are not native users of ASL, but rather are either near-native language learners of ASL or late learners of the language.[7] Regardless, we will stick to using the simple, straightforward term *Deaf* for the ASL-signing community. The term *hearing* is commonly used in the field to refer to those people who are not Deaf, so we will use this term for members of the English-speaking community.

Third, there are various terms that interpreters use to refer to the two primary roles that they perform when working as a team. The person who is currently producing the interpretation is sometimes called the "on" interpreter, the working interpreter, the interpreter in the hot seat, the target interpreter, or the interpreter in the lead role. The person who is currently working with this interpreter, but is not producing the interpretation, is sometimes called the "off" interpreter, the backup interpreter, the interpreter in the cold seat, the "feed" interpreter, the support interpreter, or the interpreter in the monitor role. To be consistent, this book uses the phrases *the interpreter in the lead role* and *the lead interpreter* for the interpreter who is functioning in the role of producing the target language rendition and the phrases *the interpreter in the monitor role* and *the monitor interpreter* for the interpreter who is functioning in the role of monitoring and working with the lead interpreter (this is in keeping with Cokely and Hawkins). In addition, sometimes interpreters refer to a team interpreter as their "team," as in, "Michaela is my team today." To avoid confusion in the book, we only use the term *team* to refer to a team of two (or more) interpreters working together and not to a single member of the team.

Fourth, interpreters use the word *process* to refer to two different notions. For example, (1) interpreters talk about the interpreting process or the team interpreting process, and, alternatively, (2) they talk about taking time to process their work. In this book, we also use this term for these two meanings. When we discuss the interpreting process, we mean the progression of steps, or the intricacies, of going from the source language to the target language or the process of making other interpreting-related decisions, and when we discuss the team interpreting process, we mean how teams manage their work together as a team. When we talk about interpreters processing their work, the term *process* is used to mean how interpreters talk over particular issues and gain insight into their teaming work.

We will also use *process time*, rather than *lag time*, when discussing the amount of time an interpreter, or an interpreting team, uses to come up with an equivalent message in the target language. This is because the word *lag* has a negative connotation, and process time is more descriptive of how interpreters use this time, i.e., to complete the interpreting process.

Note that the first use of *process* (interpreting process and teaming process) is used exclusively as a noun, the second use of *process* (to process one's work) is used exclusively as a verb, and the third use of *process* (process time) is used exclusively as an adjective. These distinctions may be helpful to the reader.

Fifth, interpreters in a team sometimes switch roles during an interpretation for the purpose of having the monitor interpreter take on the lead interpreter role to produce the interpretation, even for a short time. In the literature, this is referred to as "taking it," "taking over," or exchanging roles. Given that "taking it" and "taking over" have negative associations related to power and control, and given that this strategy is one that a team can use to benefit the team's cooperative work, we will use the phrase *switching roles* when discussing this strategy in order to describe what the interpreters are doing.

Sixth, the word *feedback* is also used ambiguously in the literature and in the field, and can convey two different notions. Feedback can refer to the advice or criticism that is offered to someone about his or her work. It can also refer to back channeling, which includes verbal utterances such as "uh-huh" or "right," or the nodding of the head or other forms of nonverbal communication, that are used to indicate comprehension and to encourage a speaker to continue speaking. Interpreters use *feedback* in this second sense when discussing the fact that the monitor interpreter is giving them on-going feedback on their interpreting work by nodding and being attentive. They use the first sense of the word to mean providing feedback to each other on the team interpreting work. When we use the word *feedback* in this book, we refer to offering advice or criticism, and we consider *feedback* to be in direct contrast to *processing* one's work, which involves a nonjudgmental and open discussion about the work, rather than a critique of the work which traditional feedback engenders (this distinction is further laid out in Chapter 9). We avoid the use of the term *feedback* for the other meaning (back channeling) and, instead of using the term *feedback*, we discuss either the intent of such behaviors (e.g., attending) or the specific behaviors that are associated with attending to the lead interpreter (such as watching or nodding).

Seventh, interpreters use a few different terms to refer to the time they spend before an interpreting assignment to discuss their upcoming teaming work together and the time after an assignment to process their work. *Pre-conferencing, pre-session, pre-assignment session, briefing,* or *briefing meeting* are common terms for the pre-assignment discussion and *post-conferencing, post-session, post-assignment session, debriefing,* or *debriefing meeting* are common terms for the post-assignment discussion. Although some of these terms describe these sessions better than others, *briefing*, in particular, seems to be unidirectional and does not really capture the intent of these interactions between interpreters. To be consistent in this book, we use the terms *pre-assignment session,* or *pre-session*, for the conversation that occurs between the interpreters before the interpreting assignment, and *post-assignment session*, or *post-session*, for the conversation that occurs after the interpreting assignment.

Finally, *support* can be used to refer to three different concepts. It is sometimes used to convey the same meaning as the second meaning of *feedback* discussed above: the fact that the monitor interpreter is nodding and attending to the lead interpreter to provide visual feedback. It is also sometimes used to mean that the monitor interpreter is feeding information to the lead interpreter as needed, as in "I appreciate how Thom provides support when I need it." Another meaning of support is providing verbal or nonverbal encouragement, e.g., looking at someone in a positive way or saying, "You're doing a nice job." Each of these three meanings–nodding and being attentive, feeding information, and encouraging the team interpreter–represents a very different kind of support.

We actually do not use the term *support* in the book to mean any of these particular behaviors. Rather, we use *support* in two general senses. (The distinction between these two meanings of support is explored further in Chapter 6). First, we use it to refer to the general support that each of the interpreters provides to the team's efforts. This support for the team is realized in the attentiveness and engagement of the team, and involves the use of a variety of teaming strategies. Second, we use *support* to refer to the notion of *offering moral support* to the other team member by being there for that interpreter psychologically or emotionally. Offering moral support is more of a personal response to working closely with a colleague, and is distinct from teaming strategies and other forms of collaboration and interdependence that support the team's work.

The principle goal of this book is to clarify what happens when two interpreters set out to work together as a team and options teams have to enhance their team interpreting work. The results of the two studies provide a way for us to expand our understanding of the team interpreting process and to look at it in a more analytical and scientific way, as well as to better understand the "art and science" of working as a team with another professional. The THOUGHT QUESTIONS are presented as discussion points that the reader can use as stimulus questions for either journal writing or discussion (processing) with others.

Acknowledgements

I deeply appreciate the input of four people with whom I have had the privilege of processing the findings in the book, and whose contributions have been instrumental in the completion of the book. First, I wish to thank Rayne Coleman for her contributions to the videotape study, for which she served as research assistant. Our conversations were particularly helpful in the initial stages of clarifying the teaming strategies reported in Chapters 5 and 6. Second, I am grateful to Tim Kinsella, Jodi Lefort, and Lianne Moccia, who read early versions of the manuscript and discussed their thoughts on the findings, their own understanding of team interpreting more generally, and the implications of the findings on how teams work and on new directions in which the field is moving. The discussions in which we processed this information were insightful and uplifting, and I will never forget these get-togethers, as they challenged my thinking on some key topics and enriched parts of the book, especially Chapters 5, 6, and 9.

I am also indebted to the many people who participated in the two studies. They remain anonymous, but this book would not have been possible without their contributions. As a field, we owe a lot to those who give of their time to help advance the field. I hope that this book helps enrich each reader's understanding of team interpreting, and I hope that it helps to advance our understanding of team interpreting as a field. After all, the field is the culmination of all of us.

ENDNOTES

[1] See Cokely, 1992; Colonomos, 1992, 1996; Seleskovitch, 1994, respectively.

[2] Kinsella, 1997.

[3] Cokely & Hawkins, 2003.

[4] The article titled "Who Comes First: The Deaf Presenter or the Interpreter?" by Hatrak, Craft, Cundy, & Vincent, 2007, and the book *Deaf Professionals and Designated Interpreters: A New Paradigm* by Hauser, Finch, & Hauser, 2008, were also inspirational to me for similar reasons.

[5] Humphrey & Alcorn, 2007; Ladd, 2003; Lane, Hoffmeister, & Bahan, 1996; Moore & Levitan, 2003.

[6] See Ladd, 2003, for a discussion of Deafhood, which is a process by which Deaf people become increasingly more self-actualized with a Deaf identity.

[7] See, e.g., Hoza, 2007a; Mitchell & Karchmer, 2004.

CHAPTER 1

TEAM INTERPRETING:
DEFINING WHAT WE DO

*One [person] can be
a crucial ingredient on a team,
but one [person] cannot make a team.*
—Kareem Abdul-Jabbar

Interpreters often interpret alone, but there are also numerous situations in which they work in teams of two or more. Team interpreting is now common practice in the field and accounts for approximately 30% of interpreting assignments.[1] With few exceptions, interpreters in today's world expect to work in teams as part of their interpreting workload.

Many factors are considered when deciding whether or not a team is needed for a particular interpreting assignment. Team interpreting typically occurs in situations that are lengthy, are complex in nature, involve unique needs of the persons being served, or involve special physical or emotional dynamics.[2] Therefore, interpreters typically work in teams in the following types of interpreting assignments:
- meetings and classes that are over an hour long;
- advanced courses, professional conferences, high-level discussions, and large group meetings;
- assignments that involve Deaf-blind persons, persons who have certain cognitive or emotional challenges, and persons who may use non-standard or heavily accented speech or sign;
- large conferences where the ability to see and/or hear the interpretation is limited, where interpreters are positioned throughout the venue to meet everyone's needs; and
- intense psychotherapeutic sessions or situations that are highly charged.

The focus of this book is on two hearing, American Sign Language (ASL)/English interpreters working together. However, many of the principles presented in the text are applicable to teams of more than two interpreters, teams of Deaf and hearing interpreters, teams working with language pairs other than ASL and English, and multiple teams of interpreters working with more than two language pairs.

The literature on team interpreting is scant, and it primarily consists of either providing a rationale for having a team of interpreters or offering suggestions for interpreters based on the author's own experience with interpreting in teams.[3] This book aims to go beyond such anecdotal evidence and has four goals. It seeks (1) to describe a current view of team interpreting based on two studies conducted by the author, (2) to review in depth how teams can successfully work together, (3) to identify areas of teaming that we need to better understand and that require additional research, and (4) to provide questions that can facilitate discussions, or journaling, for practitioners who do this work, as well as for advanced interpreting students who are learning about team interpreting.

This chapter begins with an introduction to the changing views of team interpreting in the field. Each of these views offers a different lens through which we see the process of working in teams. The early conceptualization of team interpreting is not the current conceptualization, and what people may report as their view of team interpreting sometimes differs from how they actually work in teams. The review of the changing views of teaming culminates in a more current view of the team interpreting process.

The evidence from the two studies forms the basis of our exploration of the nature of team interpreting. One of these studies involved videotaping three interpreting teams' interpreting work and the other study was a national survey of certified interpreters. The book uses evidence from these studies to argue for a view of successful team interpreting that expands upon a widely held current view of teaming; the results indicate that interpreters are ushering in a new paradigm of team interpreting.

THOUGHT QUESTIONS 1.1
What is team interpreting?

1) Define *team interpreting* in one or two sentences.

2) How did the interpreting field conceptualize team interpreting in the early days of team interpreting?

3) How does the interpreting field conceptualize team interpreting now? And how does this conceptualization differ from its early conceptualization?

FROM INDEPENDENCE TO COLLABORATION AND INTERDEPENDENCE

Our understanding of an interpreting team's function has changed since it was first widely introduced to the field in the late 1970s and early 1980s. California State University at Northridge (CSUN) was first to use teams of interpreters in the mid-1970s in the National Leadership Training Program (NLTP), which had all-day sessions, and also used teams for the second National Symposium on Sign Language Research and Teaching (NSSLRT) held in Coronado, CA, in 1978.[4] However, Cokely and Hawkins report that, with the exception of some legal situations, the first large-scale use of teams of interpreters working in concert was at the third NSSLRT in Boston, MA, in 1980.[5]

At that time, there was an increased awareness that the quality of interpretation would degenerate after 30 minutes due to fatigue.[6] It was also during the early 1980s that there was an increased awareness of overuse syndrome, or repetitive strain injury, which is the physical pain and trauma that can result from excessive repetitive movement without rest. There was concern expressed at that time that an epidemic of overuse syndrome was hitting the interpreting field. Interpreters were learning about the early signs of physical ailments that can result from interpreting for long periods of time without rest, and were learning how to take care of their bodies and to reduce injury.[7]

An awareness of the need for team interpreting in the field resulted from this new recognition of the risk of injury. Interpreters at this time understood working as a team to mean that one interpreter was to do the actual interpreting work and the other interpreter was to rest. The resting interpreter, however, was to watch for signs of fatigue, in order to relieve the fatigued interpreter as needed.[8] The terminology used at the time reflected this perspective: the interpreter who was interpreting at the time was referred to as the "on" interpreter and the interpreter who was taking a break from interpreting was referred to as the "off" interpreter.

From this view of team interpreting, both interpreters are present, but function independently from each other and take turns performing the interpreting task. The focus from this view is not on working cooperatively on the interpreting task, but rather on relieving interpreter fatigue, and the paradigm is that of two *independent* interpreters taking turns interpreting, as illustrated in Figure 1.1.

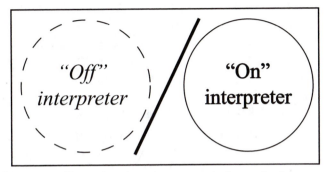

Figure 1.1. Team interpreting as an independent process:
Interpreters take turns being the "on" interpreter who is interpreting
and the "off" interpreter who is not

The goal of team interpreting soon began to shift from reducing interpreter fatigue to also ensuring the accuracy of the target language message and correcting any misinterpretations. While there was still concern about fatigue and interpreters continued to take turns at 20- to 30-minute intervals to ensure they were not hampered by fatigue, teams came to realize that they should both share the responsibility for the accuracy of the interpreted message. This led to a change in the perceived function of an interpreting team. In addition to relieving each every 20 to 30 minutes, the "feed" interpreter was expected to monitor the "on" interpreter's interpretation and feed missed information or make corrections as needed.[9] A study by Moser-Mercer, Künzli, and Korac found that errors in meaning increased dramatically after the first 30 minutes of interpreting, and that interpreters appeared to be unaware of this decline in quality and kept interpreting even though they knew ahead of time that they had the option to stop interpreting.[10]

This new view altered how interpreters framed their role as interpreters working in teams. Rather than viewing themselves as two independent practitioners who handed off the interpreting work like relay runners handing off a baton, they began to see that they had obligations to each other and the participants in the situation for the integrity of the message throughout the interpretation. This idea of feeding information that is missed or correcting information that is misconstrued, as well as being physically present in the room (as opposed to leaving the room or not attending to the other interpreter), are key components of this view of team interpreting.[11] This *monitoring view* of team interpreting is illustrated in Figure 1.2.

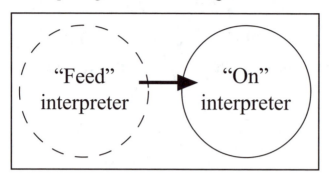

Figure 1.2. Team interpreting as a monitoring process:
The "feed" interpreter monitors and corrects the "on" interpreter's
interpretation

The literature on team interpreting is largely composed of the discussion of monitoring and feeding the "on" interpreter. As mentioned earlier, the literature is also preoccupied with justifying team interpreting, and the evidence used to support the need for team interpreting is largely anecdotal. The two primary reasons given for the need for teams of interpreters have been the two topics discussed thus far: the reduction of interpreter fatigue and the accuracy of the interpreted message.

The need for the interpreting teams to work together to ensure an equivalent target language message requires that teams determine when and how to provide feeds. Authors have stressed the need to discuss feeding styles in advance.[12] This discussion includes whether the "on" interpreter prefers to be fed whole concepts or single words/signs, or if the "on" interpreter prefers other cues such as a head nod as visual indications that the interpreter is on target with the interpretation.[13]

A pilot study by Cokely and Hawkins finds that what interpreters report as ways they will request support (i.e., feeds) differs from what they actually do in practice.[14] Cokely and Hawkins report a discrepancy between the behaviors the interpreters in a pre-interpreting session say that they will use to make such requests and the behaviors they actually use in samples of their videotaped team interpreting work. Some behaviors are quite different and others are vague in their intention, such as tilting of the head. Based on the results of this study, Cokely and Hawkins report that it is apparent that the interpreters in the study either are not fully aware of the behaviors they actually use to request support or see no need to clarify these behaviors, and interpreters may need to look at how they can more effectively ask for what they need.

Position papers of the National Association of Judicial Interpreters and Translators (NAJIT) and the Registry of Interpreters for the Deaf (RID) express this prevailing view of team interpreting as well.[15] Both stress the importance of team interpreting as a quality control mechanism used to maintain the accuracy of the interpretation, and both of these position papers discuss the fact that both members of the interpreting team are to be engaged in the interpreting process, whether in an active interpreting role or in a support/monitoring role.

A distinct voice in the literature is that of Tim Kinsella (an experienced, certified interpreter) who has expressed concern about the "feed"/"on" interpreter view of interpreting on the effectiveness and the dynamics of the interpreting team. He has stated that there is a need to move beyond correction and critique, which this view engenders.[16] In short, he states that the "feed" interpreter's role as approver and critic causes defensiveness, and this is not compatible with working in concert toward a shared goal. He urges the field to look at other models of teaming.

The NAD-RID (National Association of the Deaf-Registry of Interpreters for the Deaf) Code of Professional Conduct seems to suggest a slightly different view of team interpreting as well. The Guiding Principle under "Tenet 5.0 Respect for Colleagues" states, "Interpreters are expected to collaborate with colleagues to foster the delivery of effective interpreting services."[17] This notion of collaboration, or working jointly as a team, represents a departure from the previous two views of team interpreting. It represents a change in how the team members work together. The goal of this view is for seamless cooperation on all aspects of the team interpreting work, not just relieving each other or just feeding missed information. The goal of the collaborative view is for the team to work as one throughout the interpreting assignment.

The view that an interpreting team has of its work as a team clearly determines how the team *approaches* the task of team interpreting. If the team members assume that they are autonomous interpreters who relieve each other to reduce physical and psychological stress, they see themselves as *independent* practitioners who are taking turns doing their job. If they assume that they have an obligation to each other for the target language rendition, they see themselves as trying to work out feeds and corrections to ensure that the message is equivalent, so that the "feed" interpreter can *monitor* and *correct* the "on" interpreter's interpretation.

However, if they assume that they are collaborating to jointly create the interpretation and have obligations to each other for every aspect of the interpreting process and managing the setting and interaction, this presents yet another view: a *collaborative and interdependent* view of teaming. See Figure 1.3 for an illustration of this view of team interpreting. It is this last view of team interpreting that is the focus of this book.

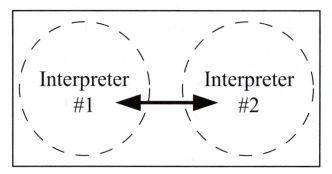

Figure 1.3. Team interpreting as a collaborative and interdependent process: Both interpreters work in partnership on their joint work

In this view of team interpreting, both members of the team work together in four major ways: (a) they relieve each other by taking turns producing the target language output, (b) they back up each other by monitoring the output, (c) they work interdependently during the interpreting work, and, (d) they work as a single unit by collaborating and making the same kinds of decisions that are made by an interpreter who is working alone. These decisions involve managing the interpreting process (e.g., determining when to begin the interpretation into the target language and when to wait for additional information), determining message equivalence (expressing the speaker's intent and the speaker's affect), and managing the interaction and other aspects of the context (such as what to do if speakers overlap their talk, dealing with making sure the environment is conducive to interpreting, and interacting with speakers when asking for clarification). The team members collaborate and pursue a shared goal, plan for how to achieve that goal, and make accommodations along the way. Crucially, both members of the team are involved in the whole process, although they may play different roles at different times. Collaboration and interdependence occur before, during, and after the interpretation itself. Collaboration begins when the interpreters first meet to prepare for the interpreting assignment and continues afterwards–often in coffee shops and parking lots–in the form of analysis and discussion of their working relationship and their teaming work.

Two other functions of team interpreting have been discussed anecdotally in the literature and are important to mention in terms of their implications for collaboration and interdependence. It has been reported, for example, that members of the team may divide up the tasks of an interpreting assignment. When interpreting in the courtroom, for instance, one interpreter may interpret the court proceedings and the other interpreter may interpret at the defense table between the defense counsel and the defendant.[18] Also, when interpreting a religious service, one interpreter may interpret the music and the other interpreter may interpret the rest of the religious service, or one may interpret the invocations of a priest or minister and the other interpret the responses from the congregation.[19] However, in these types of situations the two interpreters are interpreting at the same time for different people in the situation, so they actually are working as two *independent* interpreters, or at least as a compromised team in which each is performing a specialized function. The opportunities for truly working as a team are greatly limited because they are each focusing primarily on their own interpretations. It may well be that splitting up tasks in this way is the most effective way to provide the interpreting services in these situations and this decision could be reached as a result of agreement of the team; however, the ability to rely on each other as team members is quite limited.[20]

Others have suggested that working as a team can provide mentorship for novice interpreters, with the expressed purpose of providing feedback for the newer, less experienced interpreter.[21] However, Cokely and Hawkins' study suggests that less experienced interpreters are less likely to feed more experienced interpreters.[22] It is important that members of the interpreting team understand this phenomenon, as this inequity in feeding limits the team's ability to work cooperatively on the interpretation. The members who make up the interpreting team need to consider how the composition of the team affects the team's ability to work together to produce an interpretation. Team members should be aware of both the benefits and the limitations of this novice/mentor teaming situation and know that it will be lacking in some specific ways. It seems that most novice/mentor team interpreting situations should be confined to those situations in which the experienced interpreter could essentially work alone, and not those situations that necessitate a true interpreting team.

Team interpreting, at its core, involves two interpreters who have the basic competencies needed for the assignment and who work well together; and although interpreters may collaborate on the interpretation, only one interpreter at a time can actually produce the target language. The team of interpreters can be understood to be like copilots flying an airplane.[23] While one pilot is actually flying the plane, both pilots monitor the equipment, perform certain roles in their joint effort to fly the plane from beginning to end, make professional decisions that affect the team's work, and share the overall responsibility for a successful flight. One study found that 95% of airline crashes are due to miscommunication in the cockpit. Successful pilots take time to establish rapport with the team, are open to questions, and remind the crew of the importance of passenger safety.[24] Keys to a team effort, then, are having a clear, shared goal; having good rapport and a good, working relationship; and having a clear view of how the team can work together to successfully achieve that goal.

Interpreters can benefit from looking at how other professionals work together as teams.[25] Interpreters certainly are not pilots, but interpreters do need to maintain close, working relationships with team interpreters and to collaborate on their shared work. Miscommunication can be disastrous, and it is important to remember that we are not mind readers. As interpreters, we need to better understand how we can communicate with each other most efficiently and enhance our work together as interpreting teams.

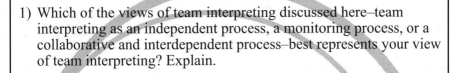

THOUGHT QUESTIONS 1.2
Views of team interpreting

1) Which of the views of team interpreting discussed here–team interpreting as an independent process, a monitoring process, or a collaborative and interdependent process–best represents your view of team interpreting? Explain.

2) Explain what you understand collaboration to mean when it comes to team interpreting.

3) Explain what you understand interdependence to mean when it comes to team interpreting (note that this term has not yet been defined in the book).

COLLABORATION AND INTERDEPENDENCE

What does it mean for a team of interpreters to *collaborate* and work *interdependently*? In this section, we explore these two terms to elaborate on this view of team interpreting.

At its most basic level, to *collaborate* means to work together to achieve a common goal. Collaboration requires people to buy into the concept of having a shared goal and making sure it is accomplished together. Therefore, having two interpreters assigned to do an interpreting assignment does not necessarily make it a collaboration. Rather, a collaborative team is the result of the actions of, and the relationship between, the interpreters involved. And the degree to which a team collaborates depends on the team members, and their ability to connect and commit to working as a team.

Now let's look at the meaning of the term *interdependence*. The best way to understand *interdependence* is to compare it to two other concepts: *dependence* and *independence*. The term *dependent* is most commonly used to describe minors or others who cannot function in some way on their own. *Dependence* implies that someone cannot stand on one's own, and that he or she needs help from others, whether the assistance is financial or comes in some other form. The concept of dependence on others seems quite incompatible with the notion of a professional. After all, being a professional presupposes a certain level of mastery and the possession of skills that presumably make the professional independent. However, all professionals are dependent on other professionals at times. Think of those instances in which an interpreter is interpreting in an unfamiliar situation and is dependent on another interpreter who works in that setting often. The interpreter who is new to the setting relies on the other interpreter to fill him or her in on the jargon, background information, and interpersonal dynamics in that setting. Without a doubt, interpreters, as well as other professionals, need to depend on each other at times. In a sense, we are all dependent on others to some degree. At the same time, being overly dependent is not a sign of a real professional.

Being *independent* means *not* dependent, of course; so being independent means being able to stand on one's own without the help of others. This is the idea behind the *independent* view of team interpreting discussed earlier, in which it is assumed that the interpreters can do the work autonomously of each other. Being overly independent--or overly dependent for that matter–does not make for a successful interpreting team. If members are so independent that they have no motivation to work with another interpreter on the interpretation, there will be little to no collaboration. Also, if either member is so dependent on the other interpreter that he or she cannot do the main tasks without confirmation or assistance from the other interpreter, then collaboration is not possible.

True collaboration in team interpreting is only possible through *interdependence*. Interdependence involves both independence and dependence. For interdependence, both interpreters should have the necessary competencies to complete the interpreting tasks independently overall, and yet they should be able to depend on each other's skills, knowledge, or expertise when necessary. Interdependence, then, involves each interpreter working independently, as possible, and relying on each other for assistance as needed. Interdependence may occur when it is requested or when it is freely given, and involves the interpreters' functioning in partnership. Interdependence requires mutual effort, good communication, a desire to look honestly at one's own abilities, and an open attitude about working together.

In short, the *collaborative and interdependent* view of team interpreting involves two main components. First, it requires that team members be committed to working together to achieve the goal of a successful interpretation, and talking through how that can best be accomplished, which requires openness and risk-taking by both interpreters, and also requires ongoing review. Second, it requires team members to have the necessary interpreting and team interpreting competencies in order to work independently as well as dependently, in order to rely on each other when necessary.

The team's approach to team interpreting is co-created by the collaboration of the team members, and involves some give-and-take. Collaboration is like a dance, in which the interpreters create synergy, and can result in something magnificent. Ideally, each member of the interpreting team works interdependently by sharing the work and by each contributing to the effort in different ways. Sometimes members are essentially completing the whole interpreting process without assistance; sometimes members discuss issues of equivalent meaning, interaction, and so forth; and sometimes members rely on assistance from the other interpreter for the team to be successful.

THOUGHT QUESTIONS 1.3
The field's views of team interpreting

1) Which of the views of team interpreting discussed here–team interpreting as an independent process, a monitoring process, or a collaborative and interdependent process–do you believe best represents the interpreting field's overall view of team interpreting? Explain.

2) Give (a) an example of when a team is collaborating and (b) an example of when a team is working interdependently (as opposed to working independently and dependently).

3) What are the greatest obstacles to working collaboratively and interdependently? And what can interpreters do to overcome these obstacles?

SURVEY RESULTS: DEFINING TEAM INTERPRETING

A group of two hundred, randomly selected, nationally certified interpreters were contacted to complete a survey on team interpreting. Forty-six of these interpreters responded to the survey, which represents a response rate of 23%. See Chapter 2 for more information regarding how the survey was conducted. The first open-ended question on the national survey asked respondents to define team interpreting in their own words.[26] These responses give us a window into these practitioners' perceptions regarding team interpreting. The interpreters' responses to the survey represent a mixture of the three views discussed in this chapter: team interpreting as an *independent* process, a *monitoring* process, and a *collaborative and interdependent* process. However, the majority of respondents seem to think about team interpreting from the perspective of the last two views (*monitoring* and *collaboration and interdependence*).

All of the forty-six respondents stated that teaming involves two or more interpreters working together. Sixty-five percent of the respondents (thirty respondents) also commented that the goal of teaming is to work together for the accuracy and quality of the interpretation. These two components are clearly key components of the view of team interpreting that these interpreters hold. Based on these two components, a common definition of team interpreting would be the following: *Team interpreting involves two or more interpreters working together to ensure the accuracy and quality of the interpretation.*

The responses to this question on the survey indicate that the majority of respondents see teaming as a monitoring and feeding process and, to a limited extent, as a means to reduce fatigue. However, a good number of responses also indicate a collaborative and interdependent view of teaming, which suggests that the field is in the process of moving to a new paradigm: a paradigm of collaboration and interdependence.

SURVEY FINDINGS: VIEWS OF TEAM INTERPRETING

The responses to the first two survey questions were analyzed to reveal the degree to which the respondents view interpreting in terms of an *independent, monitoring,* and *collaborative/interdependent* process. These two survey questions are the following: "Define team interpreting in your own words," and "What makes for an effective interpreting team (of two hearing interpreters)?" Given that these two questions are open-ended, respondents were free to respond as they wished, which allows us to get a good sense of how they perceive the team interpreting task.

Before discussing the findings, it is important to clarify that it was not possible to determine which view was reflected in some of the responses to these two questions. For example, consider the following two responses: "Any situation requiring two or more interpreters working. This may include, but is not limited to, an ASL interpreter and another language (spoken or signed) interpreter; two hearing ASL interpreters; one deaf/one hearing team, and/or someone providing real time captioning services," and "It is the process of two or more interpreters working together to ensure a successful communication event." Both of these descriptions provide a general sense of team interpreting, but do not highlight any particular view.

However, many of the responses do indicate particular views of teaming, and these responses were analyzed further to determine the prevalent views reflected by the respondents to the survey. For instance, the following example clearly shows a monitoring view of teaming:

> Two or more interpreters working the same job, supporting each other through feeding missed concepts, fingerspelling, numbers and many other aspects of interpreting. The support can be emotional in nature as well, building up confidence by encouragement as well as the technical aspects of interpreting.

Responses that reflect a monitoring view, in fact, account for 62% of the comments about team interpreting in response to the two questions. Two other examples that also indicate a monitoring view follow:

> Two or more interpreters working, not really ever being "off," but rather the "non-working" interpreter is constantly monitoring the interpretation of the "working" interpreter, in order to assist [the "working" interpreter] when support is needed in preserving the purity of the interpreting message.

> Working with another interpreter for an interpreting assignment: providing interpreting...and feeding information when necessary.

Most of the descriptions of team interpreting include a monitoring view of team interpreting, but many of them also represent a mixture of the monitoring view and either the independent or collaborative/interdependent view.

Comments about the independent view in particular account for only 6% of the comments about team interpreting, as occurs in the first part of the following example:

> Sometimes, the purpose of the team is for physical and mental relief but not much feeding can be done (like for a computer training when neither has a technical background). Most times, the one who is "off" needs to remain alert in order to feed the "on" interpreter.

Note that part of this description indicates an independent view (providing physical and mental relief) and part of the description indicates a monitoring/feeding view. Other comments that touch on the independent view of teaming include the following: "[we use] a team approach when the length of an assignment requires breaks from the physical task of interpreting," "interpreters share the physical workload of signing, through turn taking," "[team interpreting provides] an opportunity to switch so that one interpreter does not experience fatigue or overuse," and "[teams work together because] the nature of the work is physically and mentally fatiguing."

The collaborative and interdependent view of teaming was expressed by 32% of the descriptions of team interpreting. Such comments include the following: "Two [interpreters] actively working one assignment in a collaborative manner," "Two interpreters working in concert to deliver the best interpretation possible to consumers. This includes pre- and post-interpretation discussions," "working toward same goals. Open communication. No egos," "Clear communication with your team before, during and after the assignment. So that the interpretation can be done smoothly and accurately," "cooperate in decisions on how to work together," and "When two or more interpreters are collaborating during an interpreting assignment with the ultimate shared goal of complete accuracy of the overall work." Also, consider the following response:

> Respect for one another is essential. The interpreters need to have a shared philosophy of the actual goal– complete accuracy of the overall work and a willingness to prepare and collaborate in order to determine how the work will be effectively accomplished.

The monitoring view is the most prevalent view, with 62% of the descriptions of team interpreting reflecting the monitoring view of teaming. See Figure 1.4. It is also clear from these survey responses that many interpreters also see team members as having other obligations to each other beyond monitoring and feeding. Thirty-two percent of the survey respondents commented on the collaborative and interdependent nature of teaming. However, 6% of the respondents also commented on the independent nature of teaming. The reality, of course, is that interpreters do generally change roles every 20 to 30 minutes in order to avoid fatigue, so this view is part of the reality of the work of team interpreters. However, only one interpreter responded from a solely independent view, which indicates that the independent view is not highly held as a primary view of teaming. The majority of the interpreters (62%) discussed the monitoring aspect of teaming and a little less than one-third (32%) discussed team interpreting in terms of the collaboration and interdependence of the team.

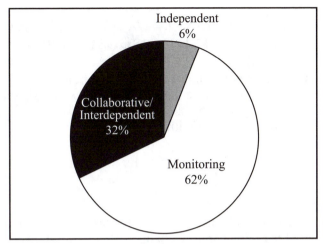

Figure 1.4. The percentage of survey responses that addressed the three views of team interpreting

The responses of these interpreters likely reflect their personal beliefs about the team interpreting process. However, it may be the case that these interpreters are simply reiterating what they have heard other interpreters say about team interpreting or they may be repeating some of the comments they received in training. Even if this is so, these comments do indicate how these interpreters are framing the task of team interpreting.

Based on this survey, the monitoring view is a primary focus in the field, which is indeed an important part of how interpreters can work together. Those who made comments about the collaborative and interdependent view often stressed that interpreting is more than monitoring, however; and those who made comments from the monitoring view often stressed that interpreting was more than relieving fatigue (which reflects more of an independent view). Of course, in reality, all three aspects are necessary components of team interpreting: teams must be aware of fatigue so that they can produce the best interpretation possible; teams must be ready to monitor and feed information, as needed, for a successful interpretation; and teams best function when they collaborate and work interdependently on all aspects of the interpreting assignment. The collaborative and interdependent view of interpreting expands on the previous views. It does not discount the other views, but rather this view builds on them. It is the next step in our understanding of what it means to be a team.

THOUGHT QUESTIONS 1.4 – Defining team interpreting
CHAPTER REVIEW AND APPLICATION

1) Identify two major points made in this chapter and write your reactions to each point. For example, you may want to discuss what these points made you think about, or you may want to discuss your agreement or disagreement with these points.

2) The purpose of this chapter was to define team interpreting. Has your own view of team interpreting changed after reading this chapter, or has it not? Explain.

3) Has the way you plan to work as part of an interpreting team altered after reading this chapter? If so, discuss specific ways in which you plan to team differently. If not, why not?

4) If one team interpreter wants to work collaboratively and interdependently and the other interpreter does not, how can the interpreters resolve this issue so that they can work effectively with each other? Or is this too big of an issue to resolve? Explain.

ENDNOTES

1 The national survey of certified interpreters, which is reported on in Chapter 2, reveals an average of 31.3% of the respondents' interpreting work involves working as a team.

2 Cohen-Gilbert & D'Entremont, 2007; Humphrey & Alcorn, 2007; RID, 2007.

3 Cokely & Hawkins, 2003.

4 Jones, 2007, citing Gary Sanderson (personal communication).

5 Cokely & Hawkins, 2003.

6 Seleskovitch, 1978.

7 Sanderson, 1987; also see AIIC Research Unit Report, 2002; Carnet, 1996; Gross, 2009, 2010; Norris, 1996; Vidal, 1997.

8 Neumann Solow, 1981.

9 Fisher, 1993; Frishberg, 1990; Stewart, Schein, & Cartwright, 1998.

10 Moser-Mercer, Künzli, & Korac, 1998.

11 Chafin Seal, 2004; Fisher, 1993; Humphrey & Alcorn, 2007; Plant-Moeller, 1991.

12 For example, Cokely and Hawkins, 2003; Plant-Moeller, 1991.

13 Fisher, 1993.

14 Cokely and Hawkins, 2003.

15 NAJIT, 2007; RID, 2007.

16 Kinsella, 1997.

17 NAD-RID Code of Professional Conduct, 2005, p. 4.

18 NAJIT, 2007.

19 Yates, 2008.

20 In the courtroom, in particular, the interpreter who is working with the prosecutor and the interpreter working at the defense table are not working as a team, but are interpreting for opposing parties.

21 Birr, 2008; Yates, 2008.

22 Cokely and Hawkin, 2003.

23 Festinger, 1999.

24 Festinger, 1999, p. 1, citing R. Ginnet, 1990.

[25] Kinsella, 1997.

[26] The participants of the other study, which involved videotaping the teams' interpreting work, were not asked to define team interpreting; however, they were asked several questions related to what constitutes an effective interpreting team and these responses are reported in subsequent chapters. See, especially, Chapter 3.

CHAPTER 2

INVESTIGATING TEAM INTERPRETING

*Teamwork is so important that it is
virtually impossible for you to reach the heights of your
capabilities...without becoming very good at it.*
—Brian Tracy

This chapter reviews the research design of the two studies that form the basis of this book. One study involved videotaping teams of interpreters interpreting the same stimulus material and interviewing the individual interpreters afterwards, and the other study was a national survey of certified interpreters who were asked about various aspects of team interpreting. The findings of the videotape study clarify three main aspects of team interpreting: (a) what the teams discussed in the pre-session prior to interpreting, (b) the interpreters' suggestions for successful team interpreting as revealed in the individual follow-up interviews, and (c) strategies that were used by the teams to support their interpreting work as a team. The survey findings further elaborate these same areas of team interpreting and further enhance our understanding of effective team interpreting.

THOUGHT QUESTIONS 2.1
Videotaping team interpreting work

1) If you were to videotape teams of interpreters to analyze their work, how would you select the teams?

2) What are the main areas of team interpreting that you would want to investigate?

STUDY #1: VIDEOTAPING AND INTERVIEWING TEAMS OF INTERPRETERS

The videotape study was a qualitative study whose purpose was to observe the work of three teams of interpreters in order to investigate effective team interpreting. Unlike quantitative research, qualitative research is less concerned with large amounts of data and reporting on the statistical significance of occurrences. Rather, the focus is on describing, interpreting, and generalizing what is observed in the behaviors of a small group of people or what is reported in open-ended interviews. Qualitative research enables the researcher to reveal strategies and explore theoretical frameworks, which is the goal of this examination of team interpreting.[1]

This study involved videotaping the pre-sessions and team interpreting samples of three teams of interpreters, and then conducting follow-up interviews with the individual interpreters afterwards. In the interviews, the interpreters were asked open-ended questions about both the team's interpreting work in the sample and their understanding of team interpreting more generally.

RESEARCH QUESTIONS

There are three main research questions that this research project sought to answer:
1. What topics/plans did the interpreting teams discuss before the interpretation, and what are some common themes among the teams?
2. What types of feeds, or other teaming strategies, did the interpreting teams use in these interpretations?
3. Based on individual follow-up interviews with the interpreters, what do the interpreters report are the key components of a successful interpreting team?

RESEARCH DESIGN

Three experienced teams of interpreters were selected by using a two-step process. First, eleven Deaf people who often work with teams of interpreters were identified and were asked via e-mail to recommend interpreters who they believe work well in a team. Of these, ten responded with their list of preferred team interpreters, resulting in a response rate of 91%. These Deaf people identified a total of thirty-three interpreters, and of these thirty-three interpreters, nine were recommended by at least half (five) of the ten Deaf people.[2]

Second, these nine interpreters were contacted via e-mail and were asked to participate in the study and to identify other interpreters with whom they prefer to team interpret. One interpreter was not available to participate in the study, but the remaining eight interpreters identified interpreters with whom they preferred to team interpret. The resulting three teams were paired up based on the fact that they had selected each other as preferred team interpreters.[3]

All three teams were videotaped interpreting into English a 42-minute ASL video on Deaf education, in which the hearing moderator, who is an experienced interpreter and interpreter educator, asks four questions of six Deaf panelists and the panelists respond.[4] This video was selected as a stimulus because the signers on the video represent a range of members of the Deaf community in terms of ethnicity, age, gender, and language usage which varies from ASL to English-influenced signing (or contact signing).[5] The video also represents a situation for which a team of interpreters is usually hired to interpret. An interpreting team typically interprets panel discussions such as this because these situations involve a substantial number of panelists, a range in language usage, and interaction among panelists and the moderator (and usually the audience).[6] These factors increase the complexity of the interpretation. In addition, the fact that the video is forty-two minutes long would ensure that the team members would need to switch roles rather than have one interpreter be responsible for producing the target language for the entire forty-two minutes.

As a warm-up, the interpreting teams watched a four-minute segment of another video on Deaf Culture that involved the same signers.[7] This allowed the teams to acquaint themselves with the range of signing style and fluency in ASL that they would encounter on the Deaf Education video. The teams also confirmed that they had never seen either of these videos before.

Each of the teams was then given fifteen minutes for discussion before they were to begin interpreting. Both the researcher and the research assistant stayed in the room during this pre-session, but they both left when the team began to interpret the stimulus material on Deaf Education. Both the pre-session and the team interpreting work were videotaped.

The teams were not told that the research was on team interpreting. Rather, they were told that the goal of the research was to capture a natural interpreting sample. The teams were informed of the purpose of the research later when each interpreter was interviewed separately, approximately two weeks after the team interpreting work. In addition, the teams were told not to discuss the interpretation with each other until after the interviews had taken place. Background questions, questions about teaming in general, and questions about this teaming assignment comprised the individual interviews. (See Appendix I.) In addition, the interpreters were shown, and asked to discuss, approximately six excerpts from their videotaped interpretation that were examples of feeds or other teaming strategies.

PARTICIPANTS

All of the participants are female and hold national certification.[8] Five of the participants are of European descent (White) and one is of African descent (Black). The interpreters had been nationally certified for a minimum of four years, with the most experienced interpreter having been certified for eleven years. At the time of this study, three of the interpreters held baccalaureate degrees, one held an associate's degree, one held an associate's degree and was nearing completion of a bachelor's degree, and the other held no degree but was working toward a bachelor's degree. All six interpreters had graduated from an interpreting program. One interpreter graduated from a bachelor's degree program, three graduated from an associate's degree program, and two graduated from a certificate program. The interpreters' ranged in age from 28 to 51. See Table 2.1.

	Team #1		Team #2		Team #3	
Age	36	51	28	33	37	41
Certified for	10 years	8 years	4 years	6 years	7 years	11 years
Interpreting Experience	14 years	14 years	6 years	6 years	11 years	21 years
Teaming Experience	14 years	10 years	6 years	6 years	11 years	10 years
Teaming with this Interpreter	10 years	10 years	4 years	4 years	6 years	6 years

Table 2.1. Information on the interpreters who comprised the three teams

---

THOUGHT QUESTIONS 2.2
Surveying interpreters

1) If you were to do a national survey of open-ended questions about team interpreting to send to randomly selected certified interpreters, what steps would you take to conduct the survey?

2) What are some questions about team interpreting you would want to ask in the survey?

STUDY #2: A NATIONAL SURVEY OF CERTIFIED INTERPRETERS

After completing the study of the three teams of interpreters, a national survey of certified interpreters was conducted. The purpose of the survey was twofold. First, the survey was conducted to provide additional information on the view of interpreting held by various interpreters across the United States, with the hope that this would enhance our understanding of how interpreters approach their work. Second, the survey was conducted to garner more information from a wider group of interpreters, in order to determine whether or not the findings of the survey could further support, or perhaps repudiate, some of the findings of the videotape study.

The survey was composed of open-ended questions that sought to elicit interpreters' perceptions, views, and expectations regarding team interpreting. The results help broaden our understanding of team interpreting and provide additional information to help inform our exploration of team interpreting. While our focus is on the overarching themes of the survey results, percentages are used throughout this book to help the reader get a better sense of the survey responses.

RESEARCH QUESTIONS

The questions on the survey sought to clarify what certified interpreters perceive as effective teaming practice in the field, and the questions focused on the following six areas (the survey appears in its entirety in Appendix II):

1. What makes for an effective interpreting team (of two hearing interpreters)?

2. What are the characteristics of an interpreter with whom these interpreters prefer to work?

3. What do these interpreters prefer to discuss–or at least have mutual agreement/understanding about–before teaming with someone?

4. What are some specific ways that these interpreters prefer to support the team's work during an interpretation, including both "feeds" and other strategies?

5. How do these interpreters expect teams to function differently (i.e., work with each other differently) depending on the interpreters and the particular context?

6. What modality and language do these interpreters tend to use to communicate during team interpreting, and why?

RESEARCH DESIGN

This study was a national, online survey of certified interpreters in the United States. Two hundred fully certified interpreters were randomly selected from the RID membership list and were contacted via e-mail with a link for the survey on team interpreting. These two hundred interpreters were chosen using the following process. First, two interpreters were randomly selected from all fifty states and the District of Columbia (51 X 2 = 102 surveys) and, second, the remaining ninety-eight surveys were sent to randomly-selected certified interpreters in states that had over one hundred RID members at the time of the survey. This approach allowed for at least two surveys to be sent to each state (and the District of Columbia), and to allow states with a greater number of RID members to have greater representation in the survey. Forty-six certified interpreters responded to the survey, resulting in a 23% response rate.

Two criteria were used to select the interpreters to participate in the study. First, only fully certified interpreters were selected. *Fully certified* was defined as holding
(a) the Certificate of Interpretation (CI) and Certificate of Transliteration (CT) (both credentials),
(b) the Comprehensive Skills Certificate (CSC),
(c) either National Association (NAD) Level IV or Level V, or
(d) National Interpreter Certification (NIC) (any of the three NIC levels).

Holding the Special Certificate: Legal (SC:L), Educational Interpreter Performance Assessment (EIPA) (4.0 or above), or Oral Transliteration Certificate (OTC) (or Oral Interpreting Certificate: Comprehensive (OIC:C)) was also considered fully certified; however, the randomly selected interpreters who held these credentials also held at least one of the other certifications listed above. Second, interpreters had to have an e-mail address, so that they could be contacted via e-mail and could access the link for the online survey.[9] If a randomly selected interpreter was not fully certified or did not have an available e-mail address, another interpreter who was fully certified and had a published e-mail address was randomly selected from the same state. In addition, if an e-mail was undeliverable, then another certified interpreter from the same state was randomly selected as a replacement.

SURVEY PARTICIPANTS

This section briefly summarizes demographic information and other data regarding the respondents to the survey. In many respects, the demographics of survey respondents reflect those of the ASL/English interpreting field as a whole.

The vast majority of respondents are female (forty-three; 93.5%) and only three are male (6.5%), and the majority are of European ancestry (forty-two; 91.3%), with only four reporting African, Asian or Pacific Islander, or Hispanic/Latino ancestry.[10] These numbers indicate what has been a trend in the field for many years: the majority of interpreters are female and of European decent.[11]

The respondents average 44 years of age and represent all regions of the United States.[12] In addition, the respondents comprise a well-educated group with many years of interpreting experience. The respondents have an average of 20.5 years of interpreting experience, and the majority of them hold a bachelor's degree or higher (thirty-two; 69.6%). All respondents are fully certified by RID, and the majority of them have been certified for over 11 years and holds more than one certification. Only about half of the respondents graduated from an interpreting program, and the majority of those graduated from certificate programs (with bachelor's degree programs coming in second).

The respondents report that, on average, 31.3% of their interpreting work involves team interpreting, which indicates the prevalence of team interpreting in the field. See Appendix III for detailed tables and charts that report on specific demographic information and other data regarding the survey participants.

THOUGHT QUESTIONS 2.3
Investigating team interpreting
CHAPTER REVIEW AND APPLICATION

1) What did you appreciate about the way the two studies were done, and what do you wish had been done differently? Explain.

2) Which research questions for study #1 (the videotape study) are you the most interested in finding out more about? What do you expect the findings to reveal?

3) Which research questions for study #2 (the survey) are you the most interested in finding out more about? What do you expect the findings to reveal?

4) What research questions, if any, were not pursued in these studies that you would like to explore further?

SUBSEQUENT CHAPTERS

The results of the two studies outlined in this chapter will be reported in the remaining chapters. The results will help us understand how teams work together, how they can change the way they work together, and how they frame their team interpreting work. The focus of our discussions in this book will be on the field's paradigm of team interpreting as evolving from an independent view to a monitoring view, to the more current view as a collaborative and interdependent process. Chapter 3 addresses what is needed for an effective interpreting team, Chapter 4 reviews the topics that are discussed during the pre-session, Chapters 5 and 6 report on strategies (types of information feeds, as well as other teaming strategies) that are used by interpreting teams, Chapter 7 discusses how teams can determine which modality and language to use when communicating with each other during their teaming work, and Chapter 8 reviews how different teams work differently due to the composition and needs of the team. Chapter 9 explores how interpreters can achieve and maintain this new paradigm of team interpreting based on collaboration and interdependence. Chapter 10 pulls together the information from the previous chapters to propose a model of team interpreting based on collaboration and interdependence, and further delineates what it takes for a team to work jointly on all aspects of an interpreting assignment.

ENDNOTES

[1]   However, percentages are used in the book to report on the number of times particular strategies are used by each of the three teams in this study.

[2]   As explained in the Preface, the capitalized word *Deaf* is used in the literature to refer to the community of ASL signers who comprise American Deaf culture and the lowercase word *deaf* is used to refer to being audiologically deaf; however, we use the term *Deaf* throughout this book. Rather than further elaborating on whether a person is "capital D" Deaf or "lower case d" deaf, we will use *Deaf* to refer to all those who use ASL, and will not make a judgment about whether particular groups of ASL signers are culturally Deaf or not. (See American Heritage Dictionary, 2001; Padden & Humphrey, 1988, 2005; Wilcox, 1989; Woodward, 1982.)

[3]   To clarify, the other two interpreters did not select each other as interpreters with whom they preferred to team interpret.

[4]   *Viewpoints 3: Deaf Education*, Cassell, 2006a.

[5]   For a discussion of contact signing, see Baker-Shenk & Cokely, 1980; Kannapell, 1993; Lane et al., 1996; Lucas & Valli, 1992; Neidle et al., 2000.

[6]   In this case, there was no interaction with the audience. All interaction was between the moderator and each individual panelist, with each person appearing alone on the screen at any time.

[7]   *Viewpoints 1: Deaf Culture*, Cassell, 2006b.

[8]   At the time of the study, five of the interpreters held both the Certificate of Interpretation and the Certificate of Transliteration (CI/CT) by the Registry of Interpreters for the Deaf (RID), and one interpreter held National Association of the Deaf (NAD) Level V certification.

[9]   SurveyCat, a secure, online survey service of the University of New Hampshire, was used to conduct the survey.

[10]   Two survey respondents (4.3%) report having Asian or Pacific Islander ancestry, one (2.2%) reports having African ancestry, one (2.2%) reports having Hispanic/Latino ancestry (this person also reports having European ancestry), and one person (2.2%) does not identify an ancestry.

[11]   See, e.g., Nettles, 2010; Stauffer, Burch, & Boone, 1999.

¹²   Also, forty-five of the forty-six respondents report that they are hearing, and one respondent reports being hard of hearing. Eight respondents (17.4%) report that they are codas (children of Deaf adults) and one respondent (2.2%) reports having other Deaf relatives.

CHAPTER 3

EFFECTIVE INTERPRETING TEAMS

*I am a member of a team, and I rely on
the team, I defer to it and sacrifice for it, because
the team, not the individual, is the ultimate champion.*
—Mia Hamm

What is considered an effective team depends on one's view of team interpreting. When interpreters take for granted that they are working independently from each other, an effective team is assumed to be two (or more) interpreters who do not need each other to complete the task at hand. When interpreters assume that they have a monitor interpreter/lead interpreter relationship, an ideal team is assumed to be made up of interpreters who know how to give and accept feeds, and have an efficient system for cueing and communicating to ensure accuracy of the target language. When interpreters assume they are working collaboratively and interdependently, the concept of what constitutes an effective team expands to include much more.

Much of the literature on team interpreting has focused on how interpreters can be supportive and encouraging of each other, and how they can provide feedback to each other.[1] Such advice goes hand in hand with a monitoring view of interpreting, in that the focus is on a hierarchical relationship between the "feed" interpreter and the "on" interpreter, with the feed interpreter in the position of evaluator and critic. Under this view, two assumptions are paramount. First is the assumption that the feed interpreter must know how to monitor, to feed information or make corrections, and to provide feedback. The other assumption is that the on interpreter must know how to take a feed, and must be open to monitoring and feedback without being defensive.

As the field moves away from the *independent* and *monitoring* views of team interpreting, the understanding of what makes for an effective interpreting team also changes. This chapter makes use of the two studies to address the question of what makes for an effective team under the *collaborative and interdependent* view of team interpreting.

THOUGHT QUESTIONS 3.1
An effective interpreting team

1) Teams can be quite effective. What are some features of teaming that are essential to effective team interpreting (under a collaborative and interdependent view of team interpreting)?

2) Teams can also not work well. What are some features that can impede an interpreting team's ability to work successfully together?

3) Think of an interpreter with whom you would ideally prefer to team interpret. What are the characteristics of this interpreter?

THE VIDEOTAPE STUDY: CHARACTERISTICS OF AN EFFECTIVE INTERPRETING TEAM

The individual follow-up interviews with the six interpreters revealed four major features that the interpreters believe make for a good team interpreter and a successful interpreting team. These areas include (a) the personal characteristics and skills of the team interpreters, (b) a shared philosophical understanding, or schema, of the interpreting process and the work of the interpreting team, (c) the interpersonal relationship between the team members and their ability to communicate well with each other, and (d) a level of trust and commitment to the teaming work and to a successful interpretation.

In the interviews, all of the interpreters mentioned personal characteristics of an ideal team interpreter. They often mentioned that they team best with an interpreter whom they like, someone who is approachable and easy to talk with, and with whom they feel there is mutual respect. They mentioned that it is best when the team interpreter is confident, but not overbearing. One interpreter referred to this connection as the *chemistry* that the members of the team need to have for the team to be successful.

In addition to these personal characteristics, the majority of the interpreters also mentioned the skills of the interpreter. These interpreters stressed it is important that the interpreter have the requisite interpreting skills as a foundation for the team to work effectively. Although these interpreters did not mention language proficiency specifically, it seems to be implied by their comments, in that interpreters must have a certain level of fluency in the relevant languages in order to interpret.

Regarding the interpersonal level, interpreters stated that it is important to know each other well and to have clear and open communication between the team members. They also mentioned the importance of not letting ego (i.e., egotism) get in the way of the team, and not feeling intimidated by the team member. They stressed the need to feel like equals, and some mentioned that it is best to work with someone who has either comparable interpreting skills or complementary skills.[2] The interpreters also felt it is important that both team members be open to feedback and discussing (processing) the teaming work afterwards. One interpreter mentioned that an interpreter may feel vulnerable when working so closely with another interpreter, but it is important for team interpreters to cope with this and to maintain an open, working relationship. Some of the interpreters stressed the importance of flexibility in the team so it can adapt to the changing needs and goals of the team, either during the same session or from assignment to assignment.

In terms of philosophy, interpreters felt that having a common view of the interpreting process and how to team together was important. Four of the interpreters said they would have a difficult time team interpreting with someone who was working under a "machine model" of interpreting, which they described as conveying literal meaning, as opposed to a deeper level of meaning.[3] Although none of the interpreters mentioned other metaphors/models of interpreting, it is apparent from their comments that these interpreters prefer to work with interpreters who are more concerned about message equivalence (conveying speakers' goals and contextual meaning) and cultural mediation than conveying merely the literal content of the message.

The interpreters also mentioned commitment and trust as being important, and these were often discussed in the context of having open communication, being able to trust that the team member will offer the necessary assistance, and knowing each other's interpreting styles and ways to best feed each other. Time was considered an important part of commitment, which includes arriving early in order to discuss the team interpreting work before the assignment begins and being available to process the interpreting work afterward. Following through on the obligation to focus on the work during the interpretation was another type of commitment mentioned, which entails being present and attentive as a team member. Commitment included a view of the message as *our* message, not *my* message; the interpreters stated the real reason for monitoring the team's work is because both interpreters create the message and both interpreters have ownership of the message. They also stated the importance of committing to learning each other's needs, as this takes time and some of this cannot be articulated.

Knowing how to back up each other as team members was highly valued by each of the interpreters, and this was often discussed in the context of devoting the time and energy to make sure this happened. All of the interpreters said that they preferred to work with interpreters who dedicate time to develop an understanding of how they can best work as a team and to learn from their team interpreting experience together.

DISCUSSION: WHAT MAKES FOR AN EFFECTIVE INTERPRETING TEAM

The interviews with the individual interpreters have revealed four features that make for effective team interpreting. The most obvious is having the requisite interpreting skills. However, team interpreters must be able to work well together as a team, so interpreting skills alone are not sufficient. Personal characteristics, philosophy, the relationship and communication between the interpreters, and the commitment and trust in each other are equally important because of the close working relationship that forms the basis for team interpreting. If a team lacks a strong connection, or the ability to "read" each other and "think alike" in some ways, the quality of the team's joint work is compromised, no matter how excellent the skills of the individual interpreters.

Two of these features involve what the team members bring as individuals to the interpreting task. The personal characteristics/skills and philosophy of each individual team member are always a given. Interpreters cannot expect others to change their personalities and skills much, yet these features are important to the success of the team. So it is wise for any interpreter to take these features into account before deciding with whom to team up for an assignment.

The other two features of an effective interpreting team have to do with the relationship between the team members and how the team members interact with each other. The relationship/communication and the commitment/trust of the team members can both be developed and honed over time to make for a more effective team. Both of these features can contribute to building familiarity, openness, and trust that are all key parts of collaboration and interdependence. See Figure 3.1 for a visual representation of these four features. These features clarify the essential ingredients of an effective interpreting team whose ultimate goal is an effective product that results from their joint effort.

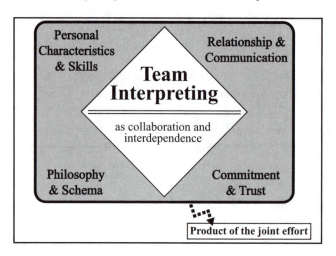

Figure 3.1. Features of collaboration and interdependence in team interpreting. The product of the joint effort of the interpreting team is dependent on the personal characteristics and skills of team members, the philosophy and schema of the team members, the interpersonal relationship and communication between them, and their commitment to the success of the team and trust in each other.

THOUGHT QUESTIONS 3.2
Four features of an effective interpreting team

1) Of the four features of an effective team discussed above--personal characteristics/skills, philosophy/schema, relationship/communication, and commitment/trust–which two are the most important? And why?

2) If you had to work with an interpreter who had only three of the four features and you could choose which one they did not have, which one could you do without? Explain your answer.

3) These features seem to imply that team interpreting involves not only a professional relationship (in terms of skills and philosophy), but to some degree a personal relationship (in terms of relationship and trust). Do you believe that a teaming relationship has both a professional and a personal aspect to it, or not? Explain.

SURVEY RESULTS: WHAT IS AN EFFECTIVE TEAM?

The question "What makes for an effective team (of two hearing interpreters)?" appears on the survey. This section reports on respondents' answers to this question, which parallel what was reported in the interviews with the six interpreters in the videotape study. In addition, the survey results help clarify which topics are given more of a priority by respondents, and the results help elaborate on some of the specifics of how these areas play out in actual team interpreting practice.

Respondents discuss four topics more than any other. The most mentioned feature of an effective team is pre- and post-assignment discussions (sixteen respondents; 34.8%). These interpreters stressed the importance of these discussions to help the team prepare for how they can best work together, as well as to help them to be aware of each person's skills, needs, and preferences; to come to a common understanding of how to best feed each other; and to discuss when they would switch (generally at 20 minute intervals). Many of these interpreters stressed that effective team members devote the time to discuss the assignment beforehand and afterwards.

The second most mentioned feature of an effective team is communication, with fifteen respondents (32.6%) mentioning good communication between the team members as an essential ingredient for an effective team. Many of these interpreters stated explicitly that this communication has to be open, honest, clear, and ongoing. One person stressed that the communication during the interpreting work must be quick and efficient. Given that pre- and post-assignment sessions are focused on communication as well, it is clear that these respondents consider the communication within the team to be important.

The third most mentioned feature is attending to the interpretation during the assignment (thirteen respondents; 28.3%). These interpreters said that both interpreters must be focused on, and actively engaged in, the interpreting work, and to be ready to assist each other when necessary. Some interpreters stressed in their responses that the interpreter who is not currently producing the interpretation needs to stay in the room and attend to the interpreting process in order to ensure that the interpretation is accurate.

The fourth most mentioned feature of effective teaming is knowing each other's strengths and weaknesses, working style, preferences, and needs, in order to best work together (eleven respondents; 23.9%). Some mentioned that it helps to know each other well, but also stated that this was not a requirement. Most of these respondents explained that knowing this information about each other helped the team adapt to their needs; to be aware of how they can compensate for, or complement, each other; and how they can best "fit" into each other's process. Some stated further that this familiarity with each other ensured that the team interpreters would be on the same page in terms of what their needs were as interpreters and how they could best work together.

In short, the four top-mentioned features of an effective team were the following:

- pre- and post-assignment discussions (sixteen respondents; 34.8%)
- good, on-going communication (fifteen respondents; 32.6%)
- engaging in the interpreting work during the assignment (thirteen respondents; 28.3%)
- knowing each other's strengths and weaknesses, working style, and needs, in order to best work together (eleven respondents; 23.9%)

Multiple interpreters also commented on other areas; these include the following. Teams work best when interpreters:

- put egos aside and are not competitive (eight respondents; 17.4%)
- are equally invested in the quality of work, and have a shared value of putting forth one's best effort (eight respondents; 17.4%)
- offer feeds, and accept feeds and feedback (without being offended) (eight respondents; 17.4%)
- are skilled and knowledgeable about the topic, and be competent interpreters and fluent in the languages (six respondents; 13%)
- are self-aware of their own strengths and weaknesses, and processing style (six respondents; 13%)
- have a shared understanding, or model/philosophy, of accessing meaning and working as a team, so they have similar expectations (five respondents; 10.9%)
- have mutual respect (four respondents; 8.7%)
- have mutual trust (four respondents; 8.7%)
- support each other throughout the interpretation (four respondents; 8.7%)

- have a good attitude, are pleasant to work with, have a sense of humor, and have the ability to relax (three respondents; 6.5%)
- collaborate and compromise (three respondents; 6.5%)
- work toward the same goals (a quality interpretation) (three respondents; 6.5%)
- provide seamless transitions without loss of meaning (three respondents; 6.5%)
- cooperate in making decisions (three respondents; 6.5%)

The survey responses echo the responses of the interpreters in the one-on-one interviews, and highlight the four features of effective teaming: personal characteristics/skills, relationship/communication, philosophy/schema, and commitment/trust. By reviewing the number of times each feature is mentioned in the survey responses, we can determine the relative overall emphasis the respondents give to each feature. Discussions of the team's relationship/communication account for just under half of these responses (45.2%) and discussions of commitment/trust account for one-third of the responses (33.5%). Clearly these two features of teaming are given the most attention in the survey. The third most mentioned feature is personal characteristics/skills (17%) and the least mentioned is philosophy/schema (4.3%).[4] See Figure 3.2. The survey responses indicate that respondents focus most on the dynamics between the team members (relationship/communication and commitment/trust). Although the other two features (personal characteristics/skills and philosophy) are mentioned far less, it may be that respondents are more likely to assume these features are present in a team, or the respondents may feel that their answers imply that team interpreters have certain characteristics/skills and a compatible philosophy/schema. It is also possible that interpreting philosophy is the least understood and, therefore, the least mentioned in the survey. Regardless of the reason, it is important to realize that all four features emerged in both studies, and are important for an effective team.

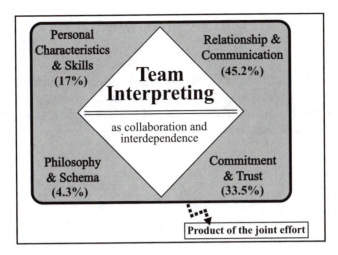

Figure 3.2. The percentages for each feature of effective team interpreting mentioned in the national interpreter survey

THOUGHT QUESTIONS 3.3
Selecting a team interpreter

1) Review the characteristics of an "ideal team interpreter" you wrote for THOUGHT QUESTIONS 3.1. Before reading the next section, determine if you would like to add any characteristics to your list or delete any characteristics.

2) Maintaining a good relationship is mentioned in the survey as a major feature of effective team interpreting. What are two key components of a good working relationship, and what are two barriers to a good working relationship?

3) Good communication is mentioned the most often in the survey as a feature of effective team interpreting. What are two key components of effective communication and what are two barriers to effective communication?

4) A team interpreter's personal characteristics/skills and philosophy/schema are mentioned the least in the survey as features of effective team interpreting. Do you agree with this ranking? Explain your answer.

SURVEY RESULTS: WHAT CHARACTERISTICS DO YOU WANT IN A TEAM INTERPRETER?

The survey also asked interpreters to respond to the following: "Describe the characteristics of an interpreter that you would prefer to work with." The responses to this question help clarify what interpreters are seeking in fellow team interpreters. The responses also provide another window into how they see the team interpreting process.

The two most frequently cited characteristics of a team member overall are similar to those mentioned by the interpreters in the videotape study, and are the following: someone who is pleasant and easy to work with, and someone who is skilled and knowledgeable. As with the other open-ended questions, interpreters worded their responses in a variety of ways and sometimes expanded on some points. We will review these responses and expansions to clarify these two main characteristics.

Most of the respondents stated that they wanted to team interpret with an interpreter who is pleasant and easy to work with; this was the most common answer to this question (twenty-nine respondents; 63%). The respondents often mentioned the upbeat personality of the person they would ideally want to work with. Having a good sense of humor was often mentioned, as well as having a level of comfort with this person-- and this was often expressed as wanting that person to be friendly, have a positive attitude (or good attitude), be amiable, and be engaging. One interpreter wrote, "friendly is always good–sense of humor is an added benefit," and another interpreter commented that "Fun is always a plus." Some mentioned that this interpreter needed to be someone they trusted, and several interpreters stressed that they wanted to feel supported by this person. One person wrote, "Sometimes the way someone comes off can block all other necessary discussions." Clearly, the personal characteristics of a team interpreter are of great importance when it comes to one's preferred team interpreter.

The team interpreter's knowledge and skills were mentioned second most often (and it came in at a close second) (twenty-six respondents; 56.5%). Most of the respondents said they prefer to work with a competent interpreter, and many also said they prefer to work with a seasoned, experienced interpreter. Knowledge was discussed in terms of life experience beyond interpreting experience, situation-specific knowledge (e.g., the participants, the material, and terminology), and knowledge about teaming. A few interpreters stated that they preferred to work with an interpreter who is well-trained and who has either comparable or superior interpreting skills to their own. A couple of people stated that they prefer to work with an interpreter who is smart/intelligent, who is analytical, and who has good diplomacy skills.

The third most mentioned characteristic was flexibility (twenty-one respondents; 45.7%). One interpreter, for example, wrote the following: "Flexibility to take on whatever is needed during the assignment." Others mentioned that the team interpreter would ideally be open to suggestions, would be cooperative and adaptable, and would be able to verbalize his or her own preferences regarding the interpreting work, but could be flexible within that.

The fourth most mentioned characteristic was a commitment to doing the best interpreting work possible (nineteen respondents; 41.3%). Words and phrases such as motivated, trustworthy, committed to the field, "willing to work with me, not against me," dependable, hardworking, focused, and helpful were all mentioned to describe the ideal team interpreter. The interpreters' view of team interpreting was often evident in their responses to this question. For example, one interpreter wrote, "someone who supports me and my sign choices as well as I support them," and some interpreters mentioned that the team interpreter should be someone who offers feeds and accepts feeds without being offended. Overall, however, the focus of the responses that fit under this category had to do with a dedication to supporting the goal of the team, which one interpreter wrote was "centered on achieving accuracy in the work."

Related to this notion of being devoted to the interpreting work, is the specific behavior of being attentive. Thirteen interpreters (28.3%) specifically mentioned that the team interpreter has to be attentive to the lead interpreter. Most of them stressed that the monitor interpreter was to be focused on the job at hand, so they are ready to provide a feed as needed. Some interpreters called this being "present in the situation." A few stressed that paying attention to each other during team interpreting shows an understanding of the benefit and scope of teaming, which is much more than switching off every 20 minutes. One interpreter said it was important that the team interpreter be focused on the work rather than the individual (i.e., focused on the process and product, not the person him/herself).

Multiple interpreters also mentioned several other characteristics. Nine interpreters (19.6%) stated a preference to work with someone who did not have a big ego, i.e., someone who was not arrogant. Some specified that the interpreter should be humble, low key, or nonjudgmental.

Eight interpreters (17.4%) used the word *professional* to describe the interpreter with whom they preferred to work. Seven interpreters (15.2%) wanted to work with an interpreter who was confident in his or her abilities, but not egotistical. One interpreter used the word *assertive* to describe the ideal team interpreter.

Six (13%) interpreters identified each of the following two characteristics: *open* and *respectful*. Those who mentioned being open, described it as being open in their approach to them as a team member and to their work as a team. One called this being collaborative and another described this as not being defensive. Those who mentioned being respectful commented on either the mutual respect of the team members or the fact that the team interpreter should have respect for participants, and especially Deaf people in the situation.

Five interpreters (10.9%) mentioned three additional characteristics. Five interpreters mentioned language fluency as an important characteristic of a team interpreter. While three of these five interpreters mentioned linguistic competence in both ASL and English, the other two only stated that the other interpreter should be a fluent signer. Five interpreters (10.9%) also mentioned the importance of the team interpreter being self-aware of his or her strengths and weaknesses (or limitations), or to be aware of each other's strengths and weaknesses. Five interpreters (10.9%) stated that this interpreter should be ethical by following the Code of Professional Conduct, with two of these interpreters stressing the importance of maintaining confidentiality.

In addition, three interpreters (6.5%) stated that this interpreter should be honest (although none of these interpreters elaborated). Also, two interpreters (4.3%) mentioned that the team interpreter should be prompt or should arrive a little early.

All of these personal characteristics and skills elaborate what these respondents believe makes for an effective team interpreter. As we see with the top two answers, an effective team member contributes to a good, trusting, and pleasant relationship, and has strong interpreting skills. Both features combine to make an ideal team interpreter. The other characteristics and skills that respondents identified in the survey highlight more specific areas that comprise these ideal characteristics and skills.

CONCLUSION

What an interpreter considers an effective team depends to some degree on one's definition of teaming. The four features of team interpreting presented here provide a framework for determining what goes into an effective team. It is clear that team interpreting goes far beyond producing an interpretation and feeding information to another interpreter.

Effective teaming is foremost about the interpreters themselves. What is important is what the interpreters can offer the team, how the team members relate to and communicate with each other, how the team members perceive how the team can function, and the commitment to see the team through the growing process of becoming a better functioning unit. Team interpreting is a professional task, but these two studies emphasize the fact that teaming entails much more than certain skills and professional judgment. Teaming is largely based on the interpreters' relationship with each other. That relationship may be more professional than personal, but it provides the foundation for the team to function. The interpreters' contributions to the team are more effectively realized when the relationship between them is a good one, and this relationship enhances the team's ability to grow as a team.

THOUGHT QUESTIONS 3.4
Further exploring effective interpreting teams
CHAPTER REVIEW AND APPLICATION

1) The survey respondents mentioned *philosophy/schema* the least of the four features of an effective team (only 4.3% of them mentioned this feature). Name two assumptions that teams may have regarding philosophy/schema when they interpret with someone new, and identify two areas related to philosophy/schema that the team would benefit from discussing before interpreting together.

2) The personal characteristics of each interpreter is important for an effective interpreting team. What personal characteristics do you bring to the team that can help the team's work, and what personal characteristics do you want to be aware of that may lessen your ability to work as a team?

3) Write down specific ways in which team interpreters can increase their trust in each other. Be sure to include specific ways in which team interpreters you have worked with build your trust.

ENDNOTES

[1] See, e.g., Plant-Moeller, 1991.

[2] Shaw, 1995, also discusses the compatibility and comfort level of the interpreters, and the desire that they have complementary skills and "knowledge of each other's skills, style, personality, knowledge level, and familiarity with the situation, subject and participants" (p. 1).

[3] These interpreters are obviously using the term *machine model* to refer to a rather literal interpretation, as discussed by Witter-Merithew, 1986, rather than Baker-Shenk's, 1992, use of this term, which primarily focuses on superficial ethical decisions.

[4] The next question on the survey asked respondents to describe the characteristics of an interpreter with whom they would prefer to work. The responses to this question are summarized in the next section of this chapter.

CHAPTER 4

THE PRE-SESSION

Teamwork is the ability to work together toward a common vision...It is the fuel that allows common people to attain uncommon results.
—Andrew Carnegie

Describing an effective teaming experience is like trying to describe a wonderful conversation you had with someone. We have all had those uplifting and exhilarating conversations that seem to naturally flow from topic to topic. Being part of an effective team is a lot like that. It is a magnificent occurrence and is one we want to happen more often once we have experienced it.

Just putting two people together in a room does not necessarily make for a wonderful conversation. Likewise, assigning two interpreters to work together does not necessarily make for an effective team. Rather, interpreters themselves create a team and sustain the team relationship, just as two people in a conversation create the conversation and maintain the interaction. Both team interpreting and maintaining a conversation involve both art and science. Conversational analysis provides tools for understanding how a conversation progresses, but it takes human beings who are in tune with each other, are savvy communicators, and know the conversational system to carry on a great conversation. Likewise, team interpreting takes interpreters who are in tune with each other, are savvy communicators, and know the team interpreting system to create an effective team.

Although interpreters may at times quickly fall into synch and work well together as a team, most of the time effective teams don't magically emerge. They require time and attention to develop. Teams generally have a starting point, they evolve, and they have check-in points along the way. One crucial check-in point is the team's session that occurs before a team interpreting assignment. The pre-assignment session is an ideal time for the team to connect with each other, to reflect on their working relationship, and to anticipate and discuss how they can work together in the upcoming assignment.

Interpreters who are working with each other for the first time often begin their working relationship in a pre-session. In addition, many of the topics discussed in a pre-session can continue to be explored after an interpreting assignment, which allows the team members to process and learn more about their work together, and to grow closer and more confident in their relationship.

Pre-sessions usually cover several specific topics. At the same time, the nature of the pre-session is specific to the interpreters and to the interpreting assignment. For example, not all topics are covered every time, and some topics may become more salient and may be focused on more in certain pre-sessions. In addition, a team may forgo discussing some topics altogether because they have a mutual understanding or agreement about those topics, which is one indication that the teaming relationship has evolved. And, of course, a certain amount of chatting takes place in the pre-session, but the amount and style of casual conversation depends to a large degree on the interpreters and their relationship. The pre-session provides an opportunity to connect with the other interpreter, to discuss important issues, and to strategize for the upcoming assignment. So, what are some of the topics interpreters discuss during the pre-session?

THOUGHT QUESTIONS 4.1
The pre-session

1) What should teams discuss in a pre-session before teaming together, or at least have mutual agreement/understanding about before teaming together?

2) What are some areas that may get overlooked in the pre-session?

3) How does the composition of the team members affect the discussion in the pre-session?

4) Identify a couple of ways in which team interpreters can establish rapport and "connect" during the pre-session.

THE VIDEOTAPE STUDY: TOPICS AND STRATEGIES DISCUSSED DURING THE PRE-SESSION

All three teams discussed the same five general topics in their pre-interpreting sessions, in order to prepare for the forthcoming interpreting assignment. However, the specifics of these topics varied to some degree for each team.

First, all three teams began the pre-interpreting session by talking about who would "take" certain participants, i.e., who would function in the lead interpreter role (and produce the interpretation) for various participants. "I'll take …," "I'll interpret for the man who…," or "Do you want to take…?" were common ways in which they discussed this aspect of their work. The decisions regarding who would be the lead interpreter for various participants was generally based on which participants the interpreters felt more comfortable with, which was often based on the particular participant's signing style. Two teams planned to have one team member consistently interpret for the moderator, and to have the two of them alternate between responses. The other team decided to alternate between all of the signers, with neither of them consistently interpreting for the moderator. All three teams also briefly discussed in the pre-session who would begin interpreting (i.e., start in the lead interpreter role). Two teams discussed this near the end of the pre-session and the other team discussed this near the beginning of the pre-session. This part of the discussion began with one interpreter asking, "Do you want to start?"

Second, the teams discussed the context and considerations for producing a message that would be equivalent in the target language. They primarily focused on the topic (Deaf education), the audience (a college presentation that is open to the public), and possible expansions or cultural adjustments. Teams #1 and #2 spoke in a general way about these aspects of the interpreting assignment. However, team #3 discussed specific options for wording that could be used in the target language (TL) rendition. For example, they discussed the likelihood that they would need to make sure that culturally rich realities such as DEAF^INSTITUTE and HEARING are conveyed appropriately in the TL, that it is best to address people by their first names in the TL to signal a connection with the audience, and that they wanted to be sure to remember to use the collective "we" when they saw the ME sign used in the source language (SL).[1]

Third, all three teams discussed how to feed information to each other. Both members of team #1 mentioned that they tend to lean in when they want a feed, and agreed that if they were leaning and the lean was not seen, they would need to tap the team interpreter on the arm for a feed. Team #2 also talked about leaning to request a feed. Team #3 talked about writing down information in order to communicate during the interpretation, and requested paper for this purpose. This was the only team that used written notes, and their notes are discussed below.

In addition to feeds, the teams also discussed other aspects of their working together. Teams #1 and #3 discussed what to do if they get stuck or miss something. These teams also discussed the fact that there may be times when it is best for the other interpreter to "take it." Team #2 did not discuss these two aspects of their teaming work, but did discuss the possibility of switching the participants for which they would serve as lead interpreter, if needed.

Fourth, the teams discussed how they tend to process information, and mentioned specific needs they have or reminders that may be helpful to them. Team #1, for example, discussed the possible need to be reminded to wait before producing the interpretation; to monitor the affect in the TL; and to be reminded to watch wording, so as not to be too literal or voice glosses in the TL. Team #2 did not discuss their interpreting process, but did discuss wanting to be told if they were talking too loudly or too softly, or making other noise (such as clicking fingernails) due to nervousness. Team #3 mostly discussed decision-making regarding conveying the message cross-culturally, such as how the discussion of the common Deaf experience in education can be conveyed to a non-Deaf audience, and making the interaction seem as natural as possible, by addressing people by name and clearly relating an answer to the question being asked.

Fifth, the topic of the seating arrangement occurred either near the beginning (for team #1) or at the end of the pre-session (for teams #2 and #3). Although chairs had been set up next to each other, teams #1 and #3 moved the chairs closer together by a few inches before beginning the interpretation. Team #2 did not move the chairs, but stated that since they could lean in to be closer, the chairs were fine where they were.

In addition to these topics, all three teams provided moral support to each other during the pre-session. This support consisted of comments the interpreters made to reassure each other about their ability to successfully complete the task. For example, the interpreters in these teams said the following to provide moral support to each other: "We'll do fine," "Let's go for it and see what happens" (both smile), and "Are you good?" (both smile and nod).

DISCUSSION: TOPICS AND STRATEGIES DISCUSSED DURING THE PRE-SESSION

The teams did not confine themselves to discussing feeds or avoiding fatigue, as would be suggested by either an *independent* or *monitoring* view of team interpreting. Rather, they discussed a variety of topics. All three teams briefly discussed how they can feed each other information, but they also talked about other aspects of the team interpreting work. These topics include how they can convey message equivalence and mediate cultural differences, how they can coordinate the interpretation of the seven people who appear on the video, what needs they wanted the other interpreter to be aware of and to monitor, who will begin in the lead interpreter role, and how they can give each other reminders. They also provided moral support to each other.

The teams touch on all four types of demands (challenges) that interpreters manage on the job, as delineated by Demand-Control Schema: paralinguistic, environmental, interpersonal, and intrapersonal.[2] Teams of interpreters may discuss the *paralinguistic* demands of participants' communication styles (rate, clarity, etc.), as well as the interpreter's language competencies; the *environmental* demands of the nature of the assignment and the seating arrangement; the *interpersonal* demands of the dynamics of the panel and each interpreter's role expectations; and the *intrapersonal* demands regarding their ability to perform the interpreting task, e.g., their nervousness about the task. These demands of interpreting assignments are the same as they are for a single interpreter; however, interpreting teams need to additionally coordinate their work as a team, which creates another demand. On the other hand, the team members can provide additional controls (resources) to help meet the variety of demands of the assignment and to support each other in their work.

The topics discussed in the pre-session make clear that collaboration and interdependence begin well before the interpreting assignment commences. The pre-sessions also highlight that there is much more to team interpreting than establishing how to "feed" each other. Teams establish (or strengthen) their working relationship, clarify how they can work together, and may discuss various demands of the assignment (paralinguistic, environmental, interpersonal, and intrapersonal).

THOUGHT QUESTIONS 4.2
Making the most of the pre-session

1) What aspects of the context do you like to discuss with a team interpreter during the pre-session?

2) Identify some specific demands (challenges) from Demand-Control Schema (within the categories of *paralinguistic, environmental, interpersonal* and *intrapersonal demands*) that you want to be sure to discuss during the pre-session.

3) Identify some controls (resources) from Demand-Control Schema (within the categories of *paralinguistic, environmental, interpersonal* and *intrapersonal controls*) that you want to be sure to discuss during the pre-session.

SURVEY RESULTS: TOPICS AND STRATEGIES DISCUSSED DURING THE PRE-SESSION

Respondents to the online survey were asked, "What should teams discuss—or at least have mutual agreement/understanding about—before teaming together?" Their responses focused on six primary areas. The top five are the same as the areas discussed by the interpreters in the videotaped pre-sessions. One area (offering moral support) was observed in the videotape study, but was not mentioned in the survey responses, and an additional area (discussing feedback afterwards) was mentioned in the survey although it was not observed in the videotape study. The survey responses elaborate on several areas and also provide more insight into the view of interpreting that these interpreters hold.

Respondents mentioned two topics more than any other. First, most of the interpreters (forty respondents; 87%) mentioned the benefit of discussing signals for feeding and asking for a feed, or to signal for some kind of help (such as needing specific information or needing a break), so that the team has agreed-upon cues to work most effectively. A few interpreters also mentioned the importance of settling on a method of communication and providing a supportive work environment. Interpreters mentioned a variety of techniques and signals that can be used. They mentioned visual cues (with leaning being mentioned the most), auditory (either whispering in private or speaking which would be audible to the participants in the room), writing on a notepad, and tapping on the knee (which was mentioned as a possibility by one person). Several interpreters mentioned that each person is different, so it is important to work together to determine what system of cues would work best for the team. The goal of signaling was to ensure an accurate target language rendition. The focus was on monitoring the target language and, as stated by some interpreters, the lead interpreter should readily admit to and correct mistakes. As one interpreter wrote, "good enough is not an option." Although one interpreter wrote, "deaf people are part of the process," the other interpreters focused only on the cueing system, communication, and support between the team members.

Second, a great majority of the interpreters (thirty-eight respondents; 82.6%) discussed the rotation of interpreters, sometimes referred to as turn-taking or switching. The focus of this discussion of rotation was on three specific areas. First, this was sometimes discussed in terms of the time each person was to be in the lead interpreter role. Most interpreters mentioned that the length of a turn tends to be from 20 to 30 minutes long (one person stated 15-20 minutes) and some interpreters stated that the length of a turn may be dependent on the specifics of the situation. For example, some said that interpreters tend to switch at natural breaks or may stay in their roles for an entire presentation, and there was a sense that there was an effort to determine what would be least disruptive for those depending on the interpretation and yet most efficient for the interpreters. A couple of interpreters stressed that a turn is never a set time (e.g., 20 minutes) because the team should be sensitive to natural breaks in discourse. Second, some interpreters discussed the logistics of switching, i.e., where the interpreters would be seated or standing and how they would physically switch places. Third, some interpreters focused on the equity of turns, in that the primary task of interpreting (being in the lead interpreter role) should be equally divided between the interpreters. One interpreter, for example, wrote that the interpreters should come to an "agreement as to what is 'fair'."

The third most mentioned topic, which was cited by twenty-six interpreters (56.5%), was the fact that the interpreters need to prepare together. This was a broad category and the respondents mentioned a variety of components that comprise preparation. Many of the interpreters mentioned that interpreters should discuss their own skills and knowledge in terms of the particular interpreting assignment. For example, some interpreters mentioned that the interpreters should discuss their knowledge of the subject, participants, and any relevant background, including specialized vocabulary. This information can help the interpreters determine who should be the lead interpreter for various parts of the interpreting assignment. Some stressed that the interpreters need to discuss the language preference of the Deaf participant(s) and to establish what signs to use for particular concepts, especially for jargon or technical terms.[3] Some stated that reviewing and discussing materials– such as handouts, an agenda, or a copy of a PowerPoint presentation– would help them prepare, and a couple of interpreters mentioned meeting with Deaf and/or hearing participants, in order to better prepare by either getting additional information or determining language preference/needs. Two interpreters mentioned that if one interpreter has "inside information" from interpreting in the setting before, then the interpreters should discuss that information and should be aware that the interpreter without this background information may need additional support during the interpretation.

Two other topics were mentioned by one interpreter each, but are worth noting here. One interpreter mentioned that interpreters should share any day-specific information that may be good for the other interpreter to know. Such information would include having a cold (or other illness) or having to step out for a moment during the interpretation. Another interpreter mentioned that interpreters should discuss to what degree they are comfortable discussing their team interpreting work *during* the interpreting assignment.

The fourth most discussed topic was the discussion of each of the team members' strengths and weaknesses and addressing particular needs they have. This topic was mentioned by eighteen (39.1%) of the respondents, and most of these interpreters discussed the fact that it was important that the other interpreter have an idea of the areas with which the lead interpreter may require support. Some interpreters gave specific examples, such as the fact that an interpreter has a long process time; or that an interpreter may need assistance with fingerspelling, numbers, or catching names mentioned in rapid succession; or an interpreter may require support with voicing (i.e., when English is the TL). Several interpreters also mentioned that the pre-session is the time to let the other interpreter know what s/he could watch for in particular, and several stressed that it is important for interpreters to know their own needs in order to share them with the other member of the team.

The fifth most mentioned area was logistics, which was cited by fifteen (32.6%) interpreters. Some respondents mentioned the following specifics of the working conditions: placement of the interpreters, whether the interpreters were to sit or stand, lighting, seating arrangements of participants and interpreters, and placement of prep materials.

These five areas mentioned in the survey were also evident in the pre-sessions of the interpreters in videotape study. Clearly, how and when to offer a feed and other supports, how and when to switch roles (e.g., at 20 to 30 minute intervals, or at natural breaks), preparing together, sharing strengths and weaknesses (and sharing issues to watch for), and discussing preferred logistics are important features of the pre-session.

One area came up in the videotaped pre-sessions that was not mentioned in the surveys: providing moral support. Because the pre-sessions were videotaped, the researcher and research assistant were able to observe this behavior. The surveys depended on self-reporting and this did not come to mind for these interpreters. Although respondents mentioned elsewhere in the survey that they support each other by providing affirmations during the interpretation (which are discussed further in Chapter 6), no one mentioned offering moral support during the pre-session even though it is likely this happens.

There is one area that was mentioned by several survey respondents that was not observed in the videotaped pre-sessions, and that is the discussion of whether or not the interpreters want to discuss feedback afterwards. This was mentioned by seven (15.2%) interpreters, and this often included a discussion of writing notes to review later with the other interpreter. All six interpreters in the videotape study mentioned the fact that they tend to write things down to process afterwards, and all of them were disappointed to find out that they could not discuss the mock interpreting assignment until after their individual one-on-one interviews (which took place approximately two weeks after the videotaping). So, this was something that these interpreters did as a matter of course, and since they all knew each other, they had assumed that they would discuss their work in the videotape study afterwards.

Finally, three additional topics were mentioned by just two interpreters each (4.3%) and show the range of options and topics that can be considered during the pre-session. These topics are the following: (1) discuss what to do if one interpreter freezes or is lost, (2) discuss the fact that the interpreters can pick up on each other's vocabulary and/or discourse styles, so there is more consistency between the two interpreters, and (3) discuss demands and controls of the situation: environmental, interpersonal, paralinguistic, and intrapersonal.

CONCLUSION

The pre-session is an important time for the team to connect with each other and to develop a plan of action. It is also a time to start thinking through what their goals are as a team and to combine their efforts in terms of anticipating speakers' goals and how to best accomplish those goals. The pre-session is an opportunity for collaboration and much can be accomplished in these types of sessions.

THOUGHT QUESTIONS 4.3
Further exploring the pre-session
CHAPTER REVIEW AND APPLICATION

1) Identify any areas that were brought up in the videotape study or the survey that you do not tend to discuss in pre-sessions that you perhaps should.

2) Are there any areas brought up in the videotape study or the survey that you feel need not be discussed in the pre-session? Explain.

3) List specific ways in which the team can discuss each of the four features of an effective team from Chapter 3 during the pre-session. (Discuss each of these.)
    a. Personal characteristics/skills
    b. Relationship/communication
    c. Philosophy/schema
    d. Commitment/trust

4) Develop a possible list of topics to cover in the pre-session.

ENDNOTES

[1] See Cokely, 2001, for a discussion of culturally rich realities; and see Hoza, 2007b, regarding the use of naming by ASL/English interpreters.

[2] Dean & Pollard, 2001; Pollard & Dean, 2008.

[3] See Larson, 1998, for a discussion of how translators handle key words, especially when the concepts expressed by these words are unknown in the target language.

Chapter 5

Strategies for Feeding Information

Teamwork divides the task and doubles the success.
—Unknown

Interpreters use a variety of teaming strategies when they work together. This chapter and Chapter 6 review five teaming strategies that emerged in the videotape study. Three of these strategies relate to feeding information, which reflects the monitor role and this interpreter's effort to ensure that the target language is equivalent to the source language by feeding some type of information to the lead interpreter. These three strategies are examined in this chapter and are further explored by reviewing the relevant survey findings. Chapter 6 will review two other teaming strategies that are employed by interpreters, but have different functions and enhance the team's interpreting work in other ways.

THOUGHT QUESTIONS 5.1
Feeding strategies

1) What kinds of information can the monitor interpreter "feed" to the lead interpreter during team interpreting?

2) How do we decide how much to feed at any given time (a word/sign, phrase, sentence, etc.)?

3) How do we decide *when* to provide an information feed (e.g., immediately, at a good break, at the end of a speaker's turn)?

THE VIDEOTAPE STUDY: THREE STRATEGIES THAT ARE USED TO FEED INFORMATION TO THE LEAD INTERPRETER

The interpreting teams in the videotape study used five types of teaming strategies to support the collaboration and interdependence of the team, and to help achieve an effective interpretation. While two of these strategies provide other kinds of support to the team, three of these relate to the accuracy of the message by providing needed information to the lead interpreter.

TARGET LANGUAGE FEEDS

A target language feed involves providing the lead interpreter with information, so that the lead interpreter can correct or add to a target language rendition that has already been produced. The overall aim of a TL feed is to make the TL more equivalent, coherent, or accurate. TL feeds, which can also be considered *additions*, can occur during a natural pause in the interpretation or can be fed to the lead interpreter while the interpreter is still producing the interpretation.

There are two types of TL feeds: corrections and enhancements. A correction represents an effort on the part of the monitor interpreter to repair any content in the TL rendition that was omitted, added or skewed.[1] If the lead interpreter incorporates the correction into the interpretation, it is usually clear to the audience that a correction has been made because the lead interpreter has to make the correction overtly in the TL. However, sometimes the interpreter can incorporate the information from the correction into a statement that fits naturally into the interpretation and the audience is none the wiser.

Enhancements are another kind of TL feed. Instead of correcting content or facts that were misconstrued in the TL, an enhancement enriches the interpretation by assisting the lead interpreter with coming up with a dynamically equivalent interpretation in the TL, and has to do with the situational and textual meaning of the interpretation. Enhancements generally add richness or naturalness to an interpretation that is otherwise equivalent in its form. Enhancements represent an effort to deepen the meaning expressed in the TL, to make it more culturally appropriate or appropriate to the situation, or to make the discourse more natural and easier to follow.

Examples of TL feeds that are functioning as corrections:
Examples of TL feeds are <u>underlined</u> below. Text that appears in **bold** is being expressed as part of the TL; text that appears in *italics* is whispered to the other interpreter.

> Lead: **...the Franklin School...**
> Monitor: <u>*Fremont*</u>
> Lead: **Excuse me, the Fremont school.**
>
> Lead: **I would see articles or see them talking–**
> Monitor: <u>*Articulate*</u>
> Lead: **–see that they were articulate. Excuse me.**
>
> Lead: **...what it's like to work with children of a variety of ages**
> Monitor: shakes her head, looks at Lead with a solicitous look, then leans and says: <u>*Interpreters who work out in the community are better able to meet people's needs*</u>
> Lead: **interpreters who work out in the community are better able to meet people's needs.**
>
> Lead: **I've seen many kids say that my interpreter doesn't seem to understand me.**
> Monitor: <u>*I don't understand my interpreter*</u>
> Lead: **or I don't understand my interpreter. Excuse me.**
>
> Lead: **We know that many Deaf children are born to hearing parents, and they often have not ever met a hearing person before–**
> Monitor: <u>*A Deaf person*</u>
> Lead: **–a Deaf person before. Do you have any advice for those parents?**

As shown in these examples, corrections are geared toward repairing specific content. In some cases the repair has to do with the meaning of a specific lexical item, name, or phrase, e.g., the *Fremont School* (to replace the *Franklin School*), *articulate* (to replace *article*), *deaf person* (to replace *hearing person*). In some cases, the intent of the utterance overall is skewed, e.g., *interpreters who work out in the community are better able to meet people's needs* (to replace *what it's like to work with children of varying ages*), and *I don't understand my interpreter* (to replace *my interpreter doesn't seem to understand me*).

Examples of TL feeds that are functioning as enhancements:

Lead is listing specific high school classes in the TL rendition.
Monitor: <u>*Pre-college*</u>

Lead: **...and I think Deaf children suffer from that.**
Monitor: <u>*a variety of methods*</u>

Lead: **Do you have any advice for how interpreters may improve their skills?**
Monitor: <u>*and improve the effect on Deaf kids' lives*</u>

Lead looks to see that the Monitor has written the word <u>Ethnocentric</u> on the pad of paper.

The examples of enhancements go beyond repairs to content. Their goal is sometimes to provide a more natural and more dynamically equivalent term or phrase, as in the suggestion of *pre-college* (instead of listing various courses). Sometimes the enhancement has to do with clarifying a referent, as with the *variety of methods* example, which clarifies the referent of *that* and makes the discourse more cohesive. The example of the feed *and improve the effect on Deaf kids' lives* helps tie the current utterance back to the topic of the panel discussion at this point, which is that all of these aspects of education have a detrimental effect on Deaf children's lives. Without this TL feed, the audience may not fully appreciate the real benefit of having interpreters improve their skills, which is now expressed explicitly (i.e., to improve Deaf children's lives). The example of the word *ethnocentric* has more to do with capturing a theme in the TL text than it does with suggesting a particular lexical item, in that this term encapsulates an overarching idea in the SL discourse. In fact, not only did the interpreting team in the videotape study end up using this term, the term also helped frame the discourse and helped to trigger related terms that were used in the TL.

Each of the two types of TL feeds–corrections and enhancements–has a different focus. Corrections zero in on errors in conveying accurate content, and enhancements look at the larger issues of situational or cultural meaning, speaker's goal, and coherence. Both types of TL feeds represent an effort to feed information to a lead interpreter with the goal of having the lead interpreter make a change to the TL rendition which has already been produced.

CONFIRMATIONS

Confirmations also relate to meaning that has been expressed in the TL, in that the monitor interpreter verifies with a confirmation that the intent of the source language speaker is being accurately conveyed in the TL. A confirmation occurs after–or while–the lead interpreter conveys the TL rendition. A confirmation serves as a kind of reality check for the lead interpreter and helps the lead interpreter know that a particular portion of the interpretation is equivalent and successful, which allows the lead interpreter to let go of what was just said in order to move on with the rest of the interpretation. The monitor interpreter most commonly uses a nodding of the head to confirm for the lead interpreter that he or she is on track and has rendered equivalent meaning in the target language. Phrases such as "You got it" or "Nice" are sometimes also used for this purpose.

The lead interpreter sometimes explicitly asks for confirmation ("Was that right?") or leans in the direction of the monitor interpreter (often with a solicitous look), but the monitor interpreter usually offers a confirmation without any such request. The monitor interpreter may see the lead interpreter hesitate, or look uncertain or even confused, and at that point may offer a confirmation.

Examples of confirmations:

Examples of confirmations are <u>underlined</u> below. Text that appears in **bold** is being expressed as part of the TL; text that appears in *italics* is whispered to the other interpreter.

Lead (asks the Monitor):   *They're all the same?*
<u>Monitor nods and says:</u>   <u>*Yeah.*</u>

Lead's voice goes up in the TL rendition, and she leans toward the Monitor.
The Monitor nods.

The Lead leans toward the Monitor during the interpretation.
The Monitor nods.

The Lead leans toward the Monitor at the end of the interpretation.
The Monitor nods.

The Lead self-corrects: **Switzerland—Sweden**
The Monitor nods.

Lead: **In another case, they had a Deaf mother…**
Lead raises her eyebrows and leans toward Monitor.
The Monitor nods.

Monitor: **Early intervention is really the key.**
The Monitor uses the "A-OK" gesture and nods.

The Lead hesitates, and then completes the interpretation.
The Monitor nods.

Both TL feeds and confirmations occur after the lead interpreter has completed the interpreting process and has produced at least part of the TL rendition. A closer look at the cognitive steps used in the interpreting process reveals how these two types of strategies differ from other types of feeds or other teaming strategies.

The cognitive process used by interpreters to determine message equivalence of the source language (SL) in the target language (TL) has been described by interpreter educator Betty Colonomos as a three-step process: (a) *Concentrating* (C), which involves understanding the meaning of the SL text; (b) *Representing* (R), which involves mentally representing the meaning without form/words; and (c) *Planning* (P), which involves formulating how to express the TL rendition.[2] This framework is helpful in discussing the mental steps an interpreter undertakes to go from the SL to the TL.[3]

TL feeds and confirmations occur after the lead interpreter completes the interpreting process (CRP) and has produced a segment of discourse in the TL, as shown in Figure 5.1. These two types of information feeds do not occur within the interpreting (CRP) process, but the next information feed (discussed below) does. This distinction is helpful to understanding the nature of these strategies and their implications for how the team can best work interdependently.

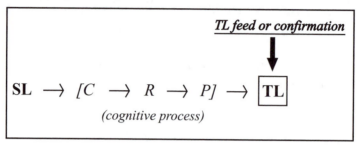

Figure 5.1. TL feeds and confirmations occur after the TL has been produced

PROCESS FEEDS

Unlike TL feeds and confirmations, process feeds are feeds that contribute to an accurate interpretation by providing an information feed to the lead interpreter *before* the TL is rendered. Most often, a process feed is in the form of information that has to do with content, but it can also relate to other aspects of a speaker's meaning, such as a cultural nuance, additional background or contextual information, a transition marker (discourse marker), the speaker's interactive intent, the speaker's affect, the speaker's goal, or the speaker's intended impact on the audience. These aspects of meaning comprise dynamic equivalence, and dynamic equivalence–not just content–can be conveyed to the lead interpreter by this type of feed, as is the case with all of the information feeds.

A process feed can occur at any point in the interpreting (CRP) process. The monitor interpreter may sense that the lead interpreter is not getting the meaning in Concentrating, is struggling with a concept in Representing, or is grappling with Planning how to express the SL meaning in the TL. Process feeds, then, represent the ability on the monitor interpreter's part to monitor the lead interpreter's cognitive processing and to assist the lead interpreter by providing information to assist the lead interpreter with C, R, or P, as shown in Figure 5.2.

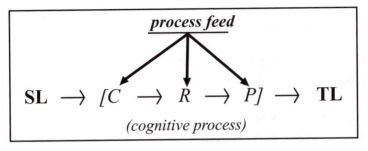

Figure 5.2. Process feeds occur during the interpreting/CRP process before the TL has been produced

The lead interpreter may signal that he or she needs a process feed, but often the monitor interpreter offers a process feed without being requested to do so. The monitor interpreter will often provide a process feed after noting the lead interpreter is pausing, hesitating, or signaling by body language or facial expression that he or she is struggling with the interpreting process. A process feed commonly consists of specific information that was missed (e.g., numbers or a fingerspelled item), contextual information that may help the lead interpreter understand the speaker's meaning more fully, the speaker's goal, or the speaker's affect.

Examples of process feeds:
Examples of process feeds are <u>underlined</u> below. Text that appears in **bold** is being expressed as part of the TL; text that appears in *italics* is whispered to the other interpreter. In each of these examples, the lead interpreter uses the fed information in the TL rendition.

Lead pauses after seeing a sign that she does not recognize in the SL.
Monitor: *<u>Fremont</u>*

Lead pauses and shakes her head after seeing fingerspelling in the SL and says: **Um**
Monitor: *<u>Fred Schreiber</u>*

Lead pauses and leans after seeing fingerspelling in the SL, and asks the Monitor: *What was that?*

Monitor: *Grassroots*

Lead hesitates and leans toward Monitor.
Monitor: *And bond with the child*

Lead pauses for six seconds.
Monitor: *They were misguided*

Lead hesitates and pauses, then looks to Monitor.
Monitor: *They were told they would be successful based on their speech*

Lead leans toward Monitor.
Monitor: *Heather Whitestone*

Lead hesitates and pauses.
Monitor: *Resources*

THOUGHT QUESTIONS 5.2
Information feeds in practice

1) Of the three types of information feeds (*TL feeds [which are either corrections or enhancements]*, *confirmations*, and *process feeds*), what feeds do you use the most? Why?

2) Are there any of these feeds that you use less often, but may benefit from using more? Explain.

3) How can interpreters best signal if they need a feed and what signals do you tend to use? What signals are more effective and what are less effective?

4) How can the monitor interpreter best convey information feeds? What is more effective and what is less effective?

5) How can the monitor interpreter best monitor the cognitive processing (CRP) of the lead interpreter, given that cognitive processing occurs in the interpreter's mind?

DISCUSSION: THREE STRATEGIES THAT ARE USED TO FEED INFORMATION TO THE LEAD INTERPRETER

The interpreting teams used five strategies to support their collaboration and interdependence as a team. Although the three strategies discussed here–TL feeds, confirmations, and process feeds–are primarily used to feed information during the interpretation, these strategies were also used during the pre-session to help the team develop a schema for the forthcoming interpretation and they may well be used in the post-session as well. For example, a correction or enhancement of information may be used during the team's schema building, a team member may confirm aspects of the jointly created schema, and one team member may provide additional information (like a process feed) during the pre-session discussion. In this sense, then, even information feeds have more of a function than to merely feed information during the actual interpreting work of the team. However, these feed strategies are most used and are most explicit when the team is interpreting together, and given the field's preoccupation with the monitoring view of team interpreting, it is little surprise that feed strategies have received the primary focus in the literature.

An analysis of the interpreting process (CRP) involved in TL feeds, confirmations, and process feeds actually clarifies how the lead interpreter and monitor interpreter may process quite differently when they are performing these roles. The lead interpreter is responsible for completing the entire interpreting (CRP) process and producing the TL rendition, as shown in Figure 5.3. The lead interpreter may also request assistance or may be offered assistance at any point in the process (during CRP or when producing the TL); it is primarily this interpreter's responsibility to decide on, and to render, the TL rendition.

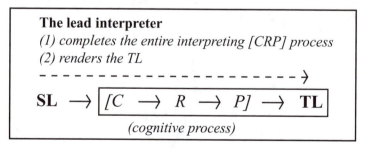

Figure 5.3. The lead interpreter's processing includes completing C, R, & P and producing the target language (TL)

The interpreter in the monitor role differs in his or her cognitive processing, in that this interpreter neither completes the entire interpreting (CRP) process nor produces the TL rendition. Rather, the monitor interpreter, generally speaking, completes both C and R, in order to have a strong sense of meaning (R), and then uses that R to monitor for TL equivalence, as shown in Figure 5.4. In this way, the monitor interpreter is not overburdened by both the need to complete the entire interpreting process and to simultaneously monitor the TL rendition and the interpreting processing of the lead interpreter. So, instead of trying to do a full interpretation and then compare that interpretation to the lead interpreter's TL rendition, the monitor interpreter stops at R and then monitors the TL rendition to determine whether or not it is equivalent to the SL (as determined by the monitor's R) or to determine if the lead interpreter needs other types of support.

By processing in this way, the interpreter in the monitor role can more freely get a sense of what the lead interpreter may need (e.g., determining if the lead interpreter may benefit from support with C, R, or P, or with the TL), can more freely attend to other kinds of communication between the team (as when the lead interpreter makes requests or the monitor interpreter makes a suggestion), and is better able to focus on different aspects of the environment or the team's needs. The interpreter in the monitor role is able to attend to these needs of the team, because he or she is focused primarily on meaning (R) and not on completing the entire interpreting (CRP) process. Thus, the monitor interpreter has the flexibility to draw his or her attention to other aspects of the team's work. See Figure 5.4.

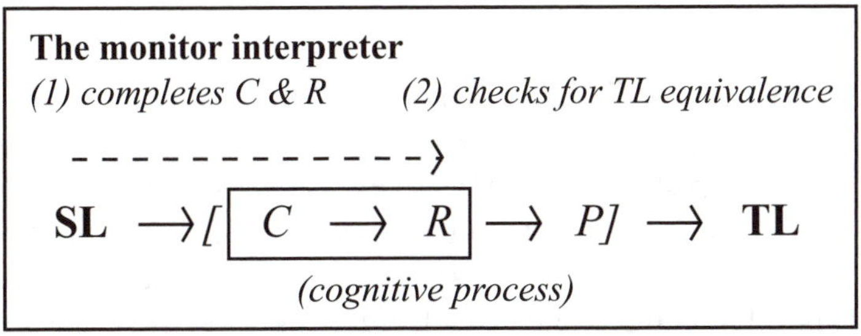

Figure 5.4. The monitor interpreter's processing involves (1) completing C and maintaining a mental representation of meaning (R), and (2) checking that the lead interpreter's TL rendition is dynamically equivalent to the SL (based on the monitor's R)

By processing in this way, the monitor interpreter can more carefully monitor the interpreting situation. The monitor interpreter, for example, can make a TL feed (correction or enhancement) by completing P and suggesting a change in the TL, can make a confirmation based on comparing the TL rendition to the monitor's own R (mental representation), or can provide a process feed (to assist the lead interpreter in C, R, or P). The monitor interpreter is also more likely to be able to provide a variety of kinds of support other than information feeds because he or she is more likely to determine needs of the lead interpreter or the team, as we will discuss further in Chapter 6.

In this study, confirmations are by far the most used feed strategy, accounting for 51.7% of the feed strategies (thirty-one of the sixty instances of feed strategies). Process feeds account for 31.7% (with nineteen process feeds) and TL feeds only account for 16.7% (with ten TL feeds). See Figure 5.5.

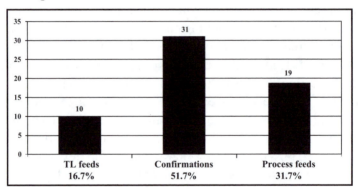

Figure 5.5. The number of instances of the three types of information feeds[4]

SURVEY RESULTS: FEED STRATEGIES

One of the questions on the survey is "What are some specific ways that a 'feed' interpreter can support the 'on' interpreter during an interpretation?" A large majority of the respondents (thirty-three respondents; 71.7%) mentioned two features in response to this question: that the monitor interpreter is to be mentally available in order to attend to the interpretation, and that the monitor interpreter is to provide feeds, as needed, to fill in missed or incorrect information. The first of these features essentially describes the overt behavior of a monitor interpreter (attending to the interpretation) and the latter describes two kinds of feeds we have identified in the videotape study: process feeds and TL feeds.

The third most mentioned feature was the use of nonverbal behaviors with the lead interpreter to convey that the interpretation is on target and the lead interpreter is getting the message (nineteen respondents; 41.3%). Nodding was the most common nonverbal indicator mentioned, but other such cues include smiling, using the thumbs-up sign, and facial responses (e.g., looking supportive). In addition, some interpreters mentioned whispering verbal indicators as well, such as "Nice," "Yep," and "Sounds good." Some interpreters also stressed that a nonverbal signal–which some called an affirmation–also supports the lead interpreter, and some interpreters mentioned the importance of having a supportive look on one's face and maintaining eye contact. Many of these behaviors can function as a confirmation.

The survey findings indicate that interpreters in the field conceptualize feeds as being of three kinds–process feeds, TL feeds and confirmations–although they may not use these terms. The findings actually help elaborate on more specific ways in which these feed strategies are realized in team interpreting. Many interpreters mentioned that repairing (correcting) errors was primarily used for missed or skewed information, and a few interpreters stressed that it was especially important to correct omissions. Many respondents also mentioned that the feed could be whispered or signed (and these two modes of communication were the most commonly mentioned). Other suggestions include writing down corrections and incorporating the correct information into a subsequent statement so as not to disrupt the flow of the interpretation. Several mentioned that the monitor interpreter could initiate the feed, but some stressed that they preferred that the lead interpreter request a feed. Most of the respondents, however, said they would provide a feed as needed, whether or not the lead interpreter asked for one.

The fourth and fifth most common responses to this question discussed (a) attending to visual information that the lead interpreter may not have access to, such as handouts or a PowerPoint presentation (ten respondents, 21.7%); and (b) monitoring the interpreting environment for other issues that may affect the work of the team, such as logistics or lighting/sound issues (eight respondents, 17.4%). Interpreters typically mentioned handouts and PowerPoint presentations as two key visual aspects of the interpretation for which the lead interpreter may need support. Some suggestions included telling the lead interpreter (by either signing or whispering) what is on a handout or PowerPoint, letting the lead interpreter know how many points are listed on a handout or PowerPoint, and showing the lead interpreter a handout and pointing to the relevant part of the handout. Other respondents mentioned other types of visual information that the monitor interpreter can report to the lead interpreter, and these include the use of a gesture by the speaker/signer, the speaker/signer making a face, and feedback from the audience, i.e., if members of the audience look confused.

Three kinds of needs–environmental, personal, and interpreting-related–comprise the types of needs that the monitor interpreter could monitor in the interpreting situation. Environmental needs include getting handouts, attending to logistics (e.g., the rearranging of furniture if necessary), adjusting the lighting, closing a door (because of too much noise coming from a hallway), and handling other distractions. Personal needs include getting water for the lead interpreter (for dry mouth), getting tissues, and adjusting a fan. Interpreting-related needs include attending to turn-taking (i.e., when different participants are speaking/signing), requesting that a speaker pause, asking a speaker for clarification, and interpreting for different participants during the interpretation.

Informing the lead interpreter about visual information is a kind of information feed strategy, and is generally a process feed, but could also function as a TL feed or confirmation. However, when the interpreter is taking care of some of environmental needs or the lead interpreter's personal needs in the situation, these are not feeds at all. These are other ways in which interpreters can work together during an interpreting assignment that do not involve feeding information. Many of the respondents seem to conflate information feeds and other kinds of teaming strategies that actually do not involve feeding information. Not all teaming strategies are feeds, as we will discuss in Chapter 6.

A handful of interpreters also identified other ways of feeding information to the lead interpreter. Note that some of these comments offer suggestions about information feeds, and some of these comments actually do not relate to feeding information. These respondents' comments include the following:

• Discuss cues for when the lead interpreter wants a feed and attend to those cues (6 respondents; 13%)
• Write notes (or use journaling) to discuss the team interpreting with the other interpreter during breaks or after the interpreting assignment (5 respondents; 10.9%)

- Take over the interpreting task (being the lead interpreter) if the lead interpreter is lost (4 respondents; 8.7%)
- Do not feed too often, as that can be too much of a distraction for the lead interpreter (4 respondents; 8.7%)[5]
- Pay attention to the lead interpreter's process time and don't jump in and feed too early (3 respondents; 6.5%)

All of these survey responses provide additional insight into the team interpreting process and highlight how complex the task of team interpreting is.

Each of the following areas were mentioned by two respondents (4.3%):
- Watch for fatigue/stress
- Use the Open Process Model of team interpreting[6]
- Always be respectful and put egos aside
- Maintain a supportive attitude

And only one respondent commented on the following areas:
- Watch for good work to laud
- Monitor the time and switch (roles) at the appropriate and agreed upon time

CONCLUSION

Teams work closely with each other to achieve a successful interpretation, and one way in which this is accomplished is when the interpreter in the monitor role provides an information feed to the lead interpreter. The videotape study reveals three types of information feeds (TL feeds, confirmations, and process feeds). The primary purpose of these feeds is to ensure that the TL rendition conveys what is intended in the SL, and information feeds represent but one way in which team members support each other's work. Some respondents to the survey, for example, seemed to identify some other teaming strategies as information feeds, so it appears that many of the strategies teams have for supporting each other are construed as "feeds" even though they do not involve feeding information. The next chapter explores two other teaming strategies that interpreters use that are not feeds, and these have different functions and enhance the team's interpreting work in other ways.

THOUGHT QUESTIONS 5.3
Further exploring information feeds
CHAPTER REVIEW AND APPLICATION

1) In addition to feeding information from the SL to the lead interpreter, the monitoring interpreter may also feed other information in the setting (such as from a handout or a PowerPoint presentation). What are other kinds of such visual (or auditory) information that a monitor interpreter may feed the lead interpreter?

2) Discuss when you, as the monitor interpreter, may not bother to offer a TL feed (correction or enhancement), confirmation, or process feed (even if it could benefit the interpretation).

3) When you are in the lead interpreter role, how do you prefer the monitor interpreter to feed a TL feed or process feed to you? That is, do you prefer to have it signed, spoken, or written, and do you prefer a single word/sign, a phrase, a sentence, or a few sentences? Explain.

4) When you are in the monitor interpreter role, how can you determine if the lead interpreter would benefit from a process feed in the C, R, or P part of the process? Explain.

ENDNOTES

¹ See Cokely, 1992, for a taxonomy of the following interpreter miscues: omissions, additions, substitutions, intrusions, and anomalies.

² Colonomos, 1996; also see Cokely, 1992; Colonomos, 1992; Seleskovitch, 1994.

³ Interpretation does not always involve a straightforward one-way rendering of a SL utterance into the TL. This is generally only the situation in formal lectures or other types of monologues. Many situations involve live back-and-forth interaction between the language users in conversations, discussions, and interviews. In these cases, the interpreter must not only constantly switch between the SLs quickly, but the interpreter also is involved in coordinating the talk, and may have more of an overt effect on the interpretation and interaction (Angelelli, 2002; Berk-Seligson, 1990; Metzger, 1999; Roy, 2000a, 2000b; Wadensjö, 1998). However, this interactive nature of interpretation is not the focus of this study, whose stimulus SL is ASL throughout and the TL is spoken English throughout.

⁴ Note that because the numbers in Figure 5.5 are rounded to the nearest tenth of a percentage point (e.g., 16 2/3 is listed as 16.7%), the total number of feed strategies comes out to 100.1%.

⁵ Two interpreters stated that the monitor interpreter should not nod too much because that can also be distracting.

⁶ The Open Process Model of team interpreting is discussed in Chapter 7.

CHAPTER 6

OTHER TEAMING STRATEGIES

A team is more than [the] people.
It is a process of give and take.
—Barbara Glacel

Working as an interpreting team involves more than monitoring the target language (TL) and feeding information. In addition to the three types of information feeds–TL feeds, confirmations, and process feeds–there are other types of strategies that interpreters can use to enhance the team's interpreting work.

THOUGHT QUESTIONS 6.1
Other teaming strategies

1) Name two ways, other than by feeding information, in which an interpreter can enhance the team's work during the interpretation.

2) What are two issues that interpreters may quickly talk over during their actual interpreting work?

THE VIDEOTAPE STUDY: TWO ADDITIONAL STRATEGIES THAT ENHANCE COLLABORATION AND INTERDEPENDENCE

Team interpreting involves a cognitively intimate and unique professional interaction between two practitioners with the purpose of providing a jointly created interpretation. Information feeds focus on specific details of a message in order to ensure accuracy, and they continue to be a focus in the field. In addition to feeds, teams use other teaming strategies that assist the team in other ways.

SWITCHING ROLES (TAKING IT)

The strategy of switching roles–or "taking it" as the interpreters in the two studies refer to it–involves the monitor interpreter and the lead interpreter exchanging roles, which results in the monitor interpreter taking the lead interpreter role by completing the interpreting (CRP) process and producing the TL rendition. Switching roles is generally temporary and typically consists of rendering a sentence or two. However, in some instances, this strategy continues and the team members stay in their new roles for a substantial amount of time.

Unlike confirmations, TL feeds, and process feeds, which clearly function as information feeds, switching roles is not a feed at all. Rather, switching roles is a way of working as a team that benefits the team by actually completing and producing the interpretation, but does not involve the feeding of information in any way. Switching roles supports the team's effort in a much different way.

Switching roles may result from a signal or overt request by the lead interpreter for the monitor to take the lead interpreter role, but the monitor interpreter sometimes just switches roles ("takes it") and begins producing the TL rendition. In the follow-up interviews, some of the interpreters said that the monitor interpreter tends to "take it" when it seems that the lead interpreter has missed too much information to adequately feed in a short amount of time. The interpreters in team #3, in particular, stated that they frequently use this strategy and often do so at the discretion of the monitor interpreter, and they generally use this strategy at the end of a natural transition point for the purpose of making the speaker's goal clearer or filling in information that may have been missed by the lead interpreter.

Examples of switching roles:
Examples of switching roles are <u>underlined</u> below. Text that appears in **bold** is being expressed as part of the TL; text that appears in *italics* is whispered to the other interpreter.

> Lead pauses, says, "**So–**," and gestures by moving her hand toward the Monitor.
> Monitor: *Do you want me to take it?*
> Lead nods, and <u>the Monitor completes the remaining 25 seconds of the current panelist's response to the moderator's question.</u>

> Lead pauses briefly while producing the interpretation.
> <u>Monitor (adds in the TL):</u> **<u>And that mother was Deaf and that child could hear.</u>**

> Lead pauses, shakes her head, leans toward the Monitor, and motions with a (palm-up) hand to the Monitor.
> <u>Monitor produces the interpretation.</u>

An information feed may not always work best for an interpreting team. There are times when having the interpreters switch roles is the most efficient means to achieve a successful interpretation.

Switching roles functions like corrections and enhancements, but does not involve feeding information. Switching roles represents another way in which team members can actively work together to produce the best interpretation possible. Whether switching roles provides a correction or an enhancement, the TL rendition is all the richer for it, and it is another strategy that allows the team to work interdependently by sharing their efforts and contributing in another way.

The follow-up interviews reveal that each of the teams views switching roles in a different way. Team #1 sees this strategy as a back-up for when an information feed is too cumbersome or time consuming to make, team #2 prefers to avoid this strategy and to only use it if asked to do so by the interpreter in the lead role, and team #3 has a preference for using this strategy at the end of a natural break to ensure a clear, cohesive, and equivalent TL rendition.[1]

Switching roles enhances the team's interpreting work by having the monitor interpreter take on the lead interpreter role and add information to the TL rendition. There is one more strategy that the teams in the videotape study used in their work together.

COLLABORATING

Collaborating involves discussing and making decisions about the interpreting work, and generally does not have to do with the relaying of meaning, *per se*. Rather, collaborating relates to how the team negotiates doing its work together. Collaborating can involve making an offer or suggestion that can help the team, such as who will interpret for whom, and either interpreter can initiate the collaboration as part of the ongoing work of the interpreting team.

During an interpretation, collaborating occurs when an interpreter makes a request such as "Will you take it?", "Was that what ___ said?", or "I missed that"; initiates a discussion by saying something like, "Should we–?"; or makes a suggestion or offers a reminder that could help the team, e.g., "Wait before you interpret."

Examples of collaborating:
Examples of collaborating are underlined below. Text that appears in **bold** is being expressed as part of the TL; text that appears in *italics* is whispered to the other interpreter.

> Lead pauses, and says: **Uh–**
> Monitor: <u>*Wait a second.*</u>
> Lead waits to interpret, then begins again.

> Lead (asks the Monitor): <u>*They are the same?*</u>
> <u>*The Monitor nods.*</u>

> <u>Lead and Monitor lean toward each other.</u>
> <u>Monitor asks Lead: *Do you want me to take it?*</u>
> <u>The Lead nods</u>, and the Monitor produces the interpretation.

> <u>Lead pauses and leans toward Monitor.</u>
> <u>Monitor to Lead: *The interpreter missed that last part.*</u>
> Lead (to the audience): **I'm sorry. The interpreter didn't get that last chunk.**

Interpreters look at each other; the Monitor asks:
   Do you want me to do Jenna [the moderator of the panel]?
Lead nods, and the Monitor completes the interpretation.

Lead (at a transition):   *Do you want me to keep going?*
Monitor nods and says: *I'll do it.*

Lead leans toward Monitor.
Monitor: *Heather Whitestone.*

Monitor leans a bit and asks: *Do you want me to take it?*
Lead nods.
Monitor says: *Okay.*
The Monitor produces the interpretation.

Lead makes a face, and motions her hand (palm up) to the Monitor.
The Monitor says, *"It's [Deaf person's name]"* [a panelist for which the
Lead prefers to interpret]
Lead begins to interpret.

Monitor taps the Lead on the arm to signal the Lead that she (the
Monitor) will produce the interpretation for the next person.

Lead asks Monitor: *What was that?*
Monitor shakes her head and says: *I don't know.*

Lead gestures with her hand that the Monitor is to take it.

These last two strategies–switching roles and collaborating–not only
occurred during the interpretation, but also emerged during the pre-session
discussion. The primary focus of a pre-session, in fact, is on collaborating.
The team focuses on how they can be successful and how they can
approach their work together. While switching roles cannot happen outside
the interpretation, two teams (teams #1 and #3) specifically mentioned it
as an option that they wanted to make use of during the interpretation.

DISCUSSION: TWO STRATEGIES THAT ENHANCE A TEAM'S COLLABORATION AND INTERDEPENDENCE

Teams have a variety of strategies that they can employ when they prepare to work together, when they interpret together, and when they process the teaming assignment afterwards. Collaboration and interdependence consist of more than spelling someone or feeding information to the lead interpreter during the interpretation. Interpreters can switch roles and they can collaborate. These strategies provide an opportunity for the team to work cooperatively for the benefit of the team without using an information feed (TL feed, confirmation, or process feed). The old adage "two heads are better than one" is at work here.

Collaborating has traditionally been understood to occur during the pre-session. In this study, we see that collaboration occurs occasionally during the interpretation as well, so that the team can iron out difficulties and to negotiate their work together. Collaborating during the interpretation occurs quickly and tends to be focused on specific issues that arise during the interpretation. Some of these issues were brought up during the pre-session, but some were not.

Switching roles allows the team to make a correction, to clarify a point, or to make an enhancement, without using an information feed. One study reports that 91% of the interpreters surveyed stated that they would "take over voicing" (switch roles) if voicing for a Deaf presenter when their team interpreter was having difficulty.[2] Reasons for switching roles include the following: the lead interpreter misses a concept, the target language message is skewed, there is a long span of silence, a Deaf presenter requests it, or efforts at feeding were not working. In addition, some interpreters reported that they would switch roles only if given the okay by the lead interpreter, e.g., only if they were asked to do so (or were nudged) by the lead interpreter.

Switching roles has some advantages and disadvantages when compared with feed strategies. Switching roles can help keep the target language on track without the need for any feeds or any disruption to the production of the target language. However, there are two important points to keep in mind regarding the switching roles strategy. First, the audience will hear two different voices (or see two different interpreters signing), which may cause some confusion for the audience in terms of identifying who is speaking/signing. This possible confusion is more of a consideration in some situations than others. Second, the two interpreters need to be comfortable with switching roles, so as not to confuse the lead interpreter who may not otherwise be expecting the monitor to switch to the lead role. In the case of the videotape study, one team clearly did not prefer this strategy and avoided it altogether; whereas, one team stated a preference for this strategy over feeding information to the lead interpreter. (We return to discuss this further in Chapter 8 when we compare how the teams in the videotape study worked differently from each other.)

Another consideration regarding the switching roles strategy is who decides if the strategy should be used. Some interpreters prefer that the lead interpreter initiate the switch in roles, and some interpreters prefer that the monitor interpreter initiate the switch in roles. Either way, this is plainly a topic the interpreters should discuss and should come to an agreement about before the interpretation begins.

In this study, collaborating was used much more often than switching roles. The collaborating strategy accounts for 86% of these two strategies (with nineteen instances), and switching roles accounts for only 14% (with three instances). See Figure 6.1.

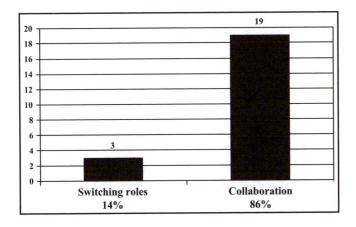

Figure 6.1. The number of instances of the two types of teaming strategies that enhance the team's interpreting work

THOUGHT QUESTIONS 6.2
Using these strategies

1) Identify which of the teaming strategies discussed in this chapter— *switching roles* or *collaborating*—you use more often. Discuss why you use this strategy more.

2) Identify which of these teaming strategies you use less often. Discuss whether or not you should use this strategy more often. Explain.

FIVE TEAMING STRATEGIES THAT SUPPORT COLLABORATION AND INTERDEPENDENCE

Of the five strategies identified in this study, confirmations occurred the most frequently with thirty-one instances of this strategy. This strategy accounts for 51.7% of the sixty *feed strategies* used and accounts for 38% of the total eighty-two *teaming strategies* used by these three interpreting teams.

The high incidence of confirmations (38%), process feeds (23%), and collaboration (23%) highlights what makes a team successful. Interpreting teams attend to both the process of arriving at the TL rendition as well as the product (TL) itself.

A confirmation provides the lead interpreter with an external monitor of the TL (product) and helps the lead interpreter to remain focused on the interpreting process and producing the TL rendition. The other two strategies, combined, account for almost one-half of the strategies used in the interpretation. Process feeds account for 23% of the teaming strategies used (nineteen out of the eighty-two teaming strategies) and collaborating also accounts for 23% of the teaming strategies used (nineteen of the eighty-two teaming strategies). Both of these strategies share a type of negotiation of the interpreting *process*. In the case of process feeds, the monitor interpreter is attending and providing information that can help the lead interpreter in that interpreter's processing of the message (i.e., CRP) in order to better arrive at a dynamically equivalent target language rendition. In the case of collaborating, an interpreter is attending to and conferring about how the team can best work together. This collaborative discussion can be about a variety of topics, but most commonly is about who will be the lead interpreter for certain participants, when to switch roles, and suggestions about processing (e.g., a suggestion to wait before beginning to interpret). Collaborating is most often initiated by a suggestion or a request by one of the interpreters.

The other two teaming strategies–switching roles and TL feeds (i.e., corrections and enhancements)–are the least used. TL feeds account for 12% of the teaming strategies used (ten of the eighty-two strategies), and switching roles accounts for 4% of the teaming strategies used (three times out of the eighty-two strategies). Each of these two strategies represents a major step taken by the interpreter in the monitor role. TL feeds involve getting the lead interpreter's attention and letting that interpreter know that what was produced in the target language was incorrect, skewed, or less coherent in some way, or that some information was omitted in the target language. The switching role strategy involves the interpreter in the monitor role producing the target language rendition and this switch will be obvious to the audience. Both of these strategies are the most overt and both of them deal with major changes to either the message or the roles each team member is assuming at the time.

All five of these teaming strategies point to the importance of a team's working closely together. The number of times collaborating and process feeds are used represent nearly half of the teaming strategies overall (46%), and these two strategies in particular focus on *process*—either the teaming process (as with collaborating) or the interpreting process (as with process feeds). This high percentage of these two strategies in particular reflects the highly process-dependent nature of teaming (see Figure 6.3). The small incidence of TL feeds and switching roles reveals that these two strategies are the most intrusive, and while important when they are needed, are used the least in the data. It may well be that TL feeds and switching roles are under-utilized by teams, and this is something for teams to explore. See Table 6.1 for a list of the total feed strategies and other support strategies, see Figure 6.2 for a pie chart that shows the percentage of the five strategies, and see Figure 6.3 for the percentage of strategies used by the three teams that are TL-related and the percentage that are process-related.

Feed strategies	*Other teaming strategies*
TL FEEDS = 10 (16.7%)	COLLABORATION = 19 (86.4%)
CONFIRMATIONS = 31 (51.7%)	SWITCH ROLES = 3 (13.6%)
PROCESS FEEDS = 19 (31.7%)	Total: 22
Total: 60	

Table 6.1. The total number of strategies by type[3]

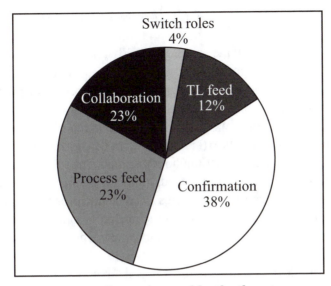

Figure 6.2. Strategies used by the three teams

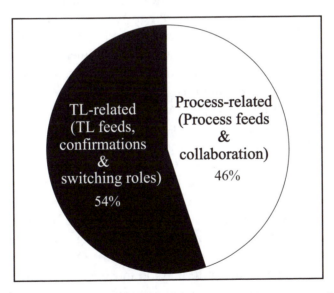

Figure 6.3. Percentage of strategies used by the three teams that are TL-related and process-related

SURVEY RESULTS: OTHER TEAMING STRATEGIES

The survey included the question, "What are some specific ways that interpreters can support each other during an interpretation–beyond 'feeding'?" One purpose of this question was to elicit responses from interpreters about teaming strategies other than feeds. A second purpose was to see if interpreters would identify other strategies, given that the focus of much of the literature (and training) to date has been on feeds; and much of the training is focused on how to signal a need for a feed, how to give a feed, how to be open to a feed, and how to incorporate it into the interpretation. The teaming strategies other than information feeds that were identified in the videotape study include collaborating and switching roles. So, what did respondents to the survey say were other strategies that teams use?

First, it is clear that ten of the forty-six respondents (21.7%) were unsure what to write in response to this question. This question about other kinds of teaming strategies followed the question, "What are some specific ways that a 'feed' interpreter can support the 'on' interpreter during an interpretation?" and nine interpreters referred to their previous answer (regarding feeds) by writing, "See above." One interpreter wrote, "How is this different from the last question?" Either these interpreters did not perceive that there were additional teaming strategies and felt they had addressed this question in the previous answer, or they found the question itself unclear. Regardless, one-fifth of the respondents, which is a large percentage of the respondents, did not answer the question.

We will now review the responses of the thirty-six (78.3%) interpreters who answered the question. By far, the most common answer to this question was to provide affirmations; twenty-three of the thirty-six respondents (63.9%) mentioned providing some type of visual or verbal affirmations. Visual affirmations include nodding, using the thumbs-up sign, body language, and facial expressions. One person mentioned that it is good to nod, but not to nod too much. Respondents mentioned verbal affirmations such as providing positive comments, professional compliments, supportive comments, saying "Nice job," or using other encouraging words. Several interpreters wrote that these affirmations are given when the lead interpreter's rendering of the TL is on target. One interpreter commented, however, that seeing the other interpreter's head nodding was "distracting and annoying; it doesn't matter if the interpreter understood, it matters if the deaf consumer understood!" Several interpreters commented that the positive support of the other interpreter was very important; such comments indicate that they see these behaviors as providing moral support (rather than as providing confirmations as we have defined them). One wrote, for example, "nothing is worse than looking down and seeing the off interpreter not being attentive or looking negative or frustrated." Offering moral support, then, is the most common response to this question. (We further discuss *offering moral support* below.)

The second most mentioned response to this question is "attending to the message." Monitoring the interpretation and the context was mentioned by fourteen of these thirty-six (38.9%) respondents. Many of these interpreters stressed that the monitor interpreter should be engaged and ready to cue the lead interpreter. One respondent stated that the monitor interpreter must be ready to take over (switch roles) at any time. Some respondents mentioned what the monitor interpreter should *not* do. For example, one commented that the monitor interpreter should not be on the cell phone or leave the room, and another wrote, "pay attention…don't read a novel or send lengthy text messages or strike up conversations with the consumer (all of which have happened to me with various teams)."

The third most mentioned response to this question was jotting down notes, with ten of these thirty-six (27.8%) respondents mentioning using notes. The interpreters mentioned two distinct functions of notes. First, some stated that notes could be used for jotting down important information, such as names, dates, facts, abbreviations, and word/sign choices (with the goal of these word/sign choices being consistently used by the team). Note that the use of notes in this way functions as an information feed. Second, some interpreters stated that the notes could be used for the purpose of discussing something that was happening during the interpreting assignment or to list specific items to process afterwards. These comments included a mention of writing down questions and comments, noting what was happening at the meeting, jotting down signed concepts that were not clear or correct, and writing feedback. This second use of notes sometimes serves as a way of collaborating (rather than as an information feed).

Six of the thirty-six interpreters (16.7%) mentioned supporting the team interpreter by making adjustments in the room. These include closing or opening a door (or window), making sure lights don't get turned off, getting handouts, holding an extra seat for the team interpreter, and providing for creature comforts such as water, coffee, or mints.

Six interpreters (16.7%) also commented on providing feedback as an additional support. Some mentioned that this usually occurs during the post-assignment session afterwards, but could also occur during the interpreting assignment (in the form of a note). The interpreters stressed the need for this feedback to be positive and that both team members need to be open to feedback. One person also warned that the interpreter giving the feedback has to be careful not to go too far with the feedback, because it could seem that the interpreter is "requiring the team [interpreter] to change things to that person's way." The two following comments highlight this sense of how feedback is to be provided: "Discuss the context and point out the positive aspects of the interpretation. Only when solicited, provide constructive feedback," and "Provide positive feedback...I always try to give other interpreters at least one positive comment about the work they are doing and I love to hear something positive about my work."

Five (13.9%) respondents commented on assisting the lead interpreter with visual information that the interpreter might miss. This included relaying to the lead interpreter that a speaker is pointing or relaying information from handouts, syllabi, or agendas. Two interpreters added that they would hold and refer to these visual materials, as needed. One interpreter added that these materials need to be "visible and in the correct order." As mentioned in Chapter 5, this strategy is actually a type of information feed.

Four other topics were mentioned in the survey. One topic was the fact that the monitor interpreter should be mindful of the timing of switches between the interpreters by paying attention to the appropriate time to switch, and should be willing to renegotiate the length of time for switches (three respondents; 8.3%). Two interpreters (5.6%) mentioned each of the following: (a) provide smooth transitions by noting vocabulary and discourse features the other interpreter is using, (b) show respect for the other interpreter, and (c) share background information with the other interpreter, as needed.

The survey results help to clarify a variety of ways in which interpreters support each other in ways other than providing information feeds. Although there are two primary teaming strategies other than information feeds–switching roles and collaborating–there are a range of ways in which interpreters enhance their teaming work. For example, one of the interpreters can hand the other interpreter an agenda or one of the interpreters can make changes to the room. All of these strategies–information feeds and other teaming strategies–help support the interdependence and collaboration of the team.

A FEW WORDS ON *MORAL SUPPORT*

A particular set of behaviors was exhibited by all three teams in the videotape study and was also mentioned in the survey as affirmations, as mentioned above. This behavior can best be described as *offering moral support,* and may be expressed by an explicit statement such as, "I know you can do it" or "You're doing great"; however, head nods and confirmations also serve to provide this kind of moral support, in that these behaviors support the morale of an individual interpreter or of the team.

Such utterances or behaviors sometimes play a dual role. For example, a confirmation such as "You got it" or "Nice" can simultaneously serve to provide *moral support* for the lead interpreter or the team, and to *confirm* that the interpretation is on track. A major difference between a confirmation and this type of moral support is that the moral support does not have to happen during the actual interpretation or even have to relate to speaker meaning. For example, moral support can occur during the pre-session, or after the interpretation (e.g., "We did a pretty good job"). This highlights the fact that providing moral support is not a teaming strategy that assists the team in achieving its goal; it is a way to help buoy up an interpreter's–or the team's–morale and to maintain a sense of emotional support. As was noted in Chapter 3, all three interpreters provided moral support at the end of the pre-session. Moral support was expressed in one of three ways in the videotape study: by the use of head nods (by all three teams), expressions such as "Nice" (primarily by team #2), and written notes (by team #3). Expressions such as "Nice," in particular, provide more moral support than head nods or the written notes, which tend to be more straightforward confirmations.

A confirmation has to do with the team interpreter's work (either the process or the product) and moral support is generally intended to buoy up the other interpreter (or the team), so that the interpreters feels better about themselves. This is like the expression, "You did a good job," that an interpreter may say to another interpreter. This phrase is generally not enlightening for an interpreter, but is intended to make the interpreter feel better.

Offering moral support, then, is a way to support the other interpreter (or the team) psychologically and emotionally. Confirmations can provide moral support, in that they confirm the successful work of the team, but offering moral support does not necessarily provide a confirmation. Confirmations represent a teaming strategy whose focus is the ongoing accuracy and effectiveness of the team's interpreting work, and moral support represents an effort to boost a person's ego.

Some interpreters may experience performance anxiety or they may feel that other interpreters are overly critical, and either of these can make them desire more support from the other interpreter.[4] In addition, interpreters may lack mastery or the necessary self-esteem for the task, and may be overly dependent on the team interpreter for affirmation and moral support. This distinction between confirmations and offering moral support is important, as the first has to do with the team's work, and the second has to do with the person's emotional or psychological needs.

The team should make sure that offering moral support to boost the ego of the other interpreter is not provided at the expense of the interpreting work or at the expense of meeting the needs of the participants in the interpreted event. The team does not benefit when the interpreters expect to be praised by the other interpreter for a job well done; the real reward is the success of the team's work.

One study by Humphrey (n = 213) found that approximately 25% of interpreters reported having experienced abuse or neglect during their upbringing, 16% of interpreters reported parental substance abuse, and 22% of interpreters reported that their parents were very strict and/ or doled out severe punishment.[5] Each of these is a characteristic of a dysfunctional family, and Humphrey warns that these interpreters may exhibit codependent behaviors such as low self-esteem, fear of rejection, relational-dependency, compulsive behaviors (such as making too many commitments), or perfectionism.

Before an interpreter can be an effective part of a team, an interpreter must be an effective interpreter. If an interpreter is expecting that any insecurities or past baggage is to be somehow managed by the team, this expectation is going to work against the team. Team interpreting is not the place to resolve personal issues. Interpreters must have a certain level of self-esteem, or ego strength, to work closely with another professional and to facilitate communication events in the lives of the primary participants. Interpreters need to be focusing on doing a good job, and should seek out other ways of getting the emotional or psychological support they need. If an interpreter feels fragile, that works against the team in this intimate task; this is not the place for the team to take care of each other's insecurities.

There are other possible reasons why an interpreter may want to receive or to give excessive moral support. It may well be that an interpreter feels anxious about an assignment. An interpreter may also feel a sense of competition with the other team interpreter, and a feeling of competition may be reinforced by his/her educational program or within the field. Several survey respondents and some of the interpreters in the one-on-one interviews stated that they preferred to team interpret with someone with "equal skills" or "comparable skills." This comment may be due in part to wanting to avoid a sense of competition. However, it must be realized that all interpreters vary in their skills, and that variation in background and skills can actually contribute to the effectiveness of the team.

There are two other reasons why interpreters may seek or offer excessive moral support. An interpreter may not know how to talk about the interpreting process or the team interpreting work, so this is a way to, at least, seem supportive of the process (by offering moral support to the other interpreter). Another reason may be a gender difference. It may be that female interpreters generally offer moral support more often than male interpreters, but further research needs to be conducted to determine to what degree this is true.

Offering affirmations and moral support can be a natural part of working closely with another professional and can help boost a team's morale. There is, however, a danger that it can work against the team if the team is overly focused on each other's feelings and insecurities, and less focused on the success of their work together.

CONCLUSION

Teams have a variety of strategies at their disposal: switching roles, collaborating, TL feeds (corrections and enhancements), confirmations, and process feeds; and they need to decide when and how to use these strategies effectively. Team interpreting requires an additional level of expertise and skill that interpreters need to develop; and using these strategies represents a major feature of a collaborative and interdependent view of team interpreting, in contrast to an independent or monitoring view of teaming.

THOUGHT QUESTIONS 6.3
Further exploring teaming strategies
CHAPTER REVIEW AND APPLICATION

1) Explain in your own words the difference between *information feeds* and *other teaming strategies*, and explain how this distinction can be helpful to an interpreting team.

2) Some of the respondents to the survey stated that some strategies can be used too often. Consider the five strategies we have discussed in these last two chapters—*TL feeds (i.e., corrections and enhancements), confirmations, process feeds, switching roles*, and *collaborating*—and give an example of when one of these strategies can be overused.

3) Are there any of these strategies that you feel the field, in general, does not use enough? Explain.

4) Are there any of these strategies that you plan to use more in your own teaming work, or less in your own teaming work? Explain.

5) Discuss your personal reaction to the section above entitled "A few words on *moral support*." Can offering moral support be helpful to the team? If so, when? Can it be detrimental to the team? If so, when?

ENDNOTES

[1]   Both of the interpreters in team #3 mentioned that they did not use the switch roles strategy in this interpretation because they could not stop the video and, therefore, they were more focused on getting as much across as they could within the imposed time constraints.

[2]   Hatrak, Craft, Cundy, & Vincent, 2007, p. 14.

[3]   As with Figure 5.5, the numbers given for feed strategies in Table 6.1 are rounded to the nearest tenth of a percentage point (16.7%, etc.); therefore, the total number of feed strategies comes out to 100.1%.

[4]   Plant-Moeller, 1991.

[5]   Kanda, 1992. Note that Janice H. Kanda is now Janice H. Humphrey.

CHAPTER 7

MODALITY AND LANGUAGE USAGE

Teamwork: Simply stated, it is less me and more we.
—Unknown

Of the five senses, three provide possible modalities for signaling and communicating during team interpreting: sight, hearing, and touch. ASL/ English interpreters can use visual communication such as nodding, using gestures, writing (in English), or using a visual language (ASL); can make sounds (clearing one's throat) or use a spoken language (English); or can use touch, e.g., tapping or patting the other interpreter on the arm or shoulder. Interpreters can use nonverbal communication or they can opt to use one of their working languages–ASL or English–to communicate with each other during the team interpreting assignment. The interpreting team may either consciously select the modality and language that works for them, or they may decide on the fly what to use at any given time. It is also likely that certain ways of communicating are more effective at different times.

THOUGHT QUESTIONS 7.1
Your own modality and language usage

1) What *modality* do you tend to use (e.g., spoken, signed, or written) to communicate with a team member during the team interpreting assignment? And why?

2) What *language* do you tend to use (e.g., English, ASL, or nonverbal communication) to communicate with a team member during the team interpreting assignment? And why?

3) What factors determine what *modality* and *language* you use with a team member at any given time?

THE VIDEOTAPE STUDY: CHOOSING A MODALITY AND LANGUAGE

When teams communicate with each other during their teaming work, they can use either the auditory or visual modality, and can use either nonverbal communication (such as body language) or one of their working languages (ASL or English). The three interpreting teams in these interpretations used the following means of communication: 1) spoken English, 2) visual nonverbal communication (body language and gestures), and 3) written English. The spoken communications took the form of whispering and, of course, written communication involved the use of English. All of the visual communication in these interpretations (other than writing) involved nonverbal communication, which included such behaviors as leaning, nodding, making a puzzled face, and looking at the other interpreter. There were also two instances of tapping the lead interpreter on the arm. However, none of the teams used ASL for the purpose of feeds or other forms of support, although the use of ASL is an option, which we discuss below.

The team can also use written notes during the interpretation. Two teams mentioned that they generally write notes to process afterwards. However, one team used them effectively during the interpretation to both feed and to offer other types of support for the team. For example, in the instance when an interpreter had written the word *ethnocentric* so that she would be sure to use the term, the team member read the word and used it in the interpretation. This exemplified one way in which this team used notes. This team saw notes as part of the team's collaboration and interdependence, in that either interpreter could use what was written, so the fact that this word was ultimately taken as a "feed" was considered good teaming. There are also several instances in which confirmations were conveyed by writing notes. Consider, for example, the following, which one interpreter wrote in her notes: *love how we drop form.* Notes were used less often for confirmations and collaboration during the interpretation. Confirmations were generally conveyed by the use of a head nod, and collaborating tended to take the form of spoken English.

The teams had a preference for three different modalities (spoken, nonverbal communication, and written), but each team used at least two of these. Teams #1 and #2 used a higher percentage of verbal communication and team #3 used a higher percentage of written communication, but all of the teams also used nonverbal communication.

THOUGHT QUESTIONS 7.2
The field's modality and language usage

1) How is the modality and language you use during a teaming assignment different or similar to the interpreters' use in the videotape study?

2) What modality and language usage do you see used most in the field? Why do you think this modality and this language are used the most?

3) Talk to other interpreters, and Deaf and hearing people with whom you work, about what modality and language usage they prefer interpreters to use when communicating with each other and why.

DISCUSSION: CHOOSING A MODALITY AND LANGUAGE

Interpreters have a few different modalities from which to choose to communicate during the interpretation, and each has different pros and cons. The spoken word, as well as the written word, can be the most explicit and clear. Nonverbal communication can be the least understood. For example, a lean or the use of nodding can be either missed or misunderstood by the other interpreter, and such signals may be ambiguous.[1] Although none of the three teams in this study used ASL feeds, one of the decisions of the team is to determine whether the communication will be in ASL or spoken English.[2]

There are likely three reasons why English was the language used by the interpreters for feeding and other teaming strategies in these interpretations. First, it may well be that the interpreters naturally gravitated toward using English because English was the target language (TL). Second, the two chairs in the videotaping space were positioned next to each other, so the interpreters may have assumed that English would be easier to use—especially given it is awkward for someone to sign to a person who is sitting very close by. Third, although Deaf people appeared in the DVD, there were no Deaf people physically present in the room. It is unclear if having a live Deaf person present would affect the interpreters' decision. So the nature of the videotaping may have affected the interpreters' choice of modality and language.

Molly R. Wilson (certified interpreter, educator, and native signer) advocates for feeds in ASL, in what she calls the Open Process Model of team interpreting.[3] In an open process, the Deaf person is included in a team's decision-making and problem-solving process through natural dialogues in ASL. In the case of voice interpreting, for example, when interpreters whisper or write their "feeds" to each other, their process is closed off to the Deaf participants and the paradigm shifts from a more collectivistic and contextualized Deaf construct to a more individualistic and decontextualized hearing one. Rather than having the interpreting process under the sole ownership/control of the interpreters, an open process extends/expands the opportunity for Deaf people to participate in, and influence the accuracy and integrity of, the interpretation delivered.

The choice of modality (visual or auditory) and the choice of language usage (ASL or English) are important for the team. These choices can affect not only the ability of the team members to support the team's efforts, but can also have an effect on the team's relationship with others in the interpreting environment. In particular, the team needs to consider how open the process should be to the Deaf participants. Keeping the support and collaboration between the interpreters may be more of a priority in some situations. However, the choice of modality and language usage needs to be a conscious decision and one that may well depend on the situation. The fact that the use of ASL for feeds, support, and negotiation includes the Deaf participants in the process is an important consideration.

It has been reported that collectivistic cultures, such as American Deaf Culture, prefer to make decisions by caucusing and negotiating as opposed to individualistic cultures, such as the majority U.S. culture, that prefer to have individuals make up their own minds.[4] I have stated in previous work that caucusing with colleagues and primary participants (especially Deaf people) in the context of ethical and professional decision-making "reflects a more collectivistic approach to decision-making, one that may seem foreign to those uncomfortable with a collectivistic cultural perspective."[5] MJ Bienvenu (Deaf professor and activist) also reports that Deaf people want the following from interpreters: "At the top of the list for us is cultural sensitivity; second is language. Perhaps last is the ability to interpret."[6] So, while interpreters spend a lot of time focusing on the nuts and bolts of team interpreting (and interpreting itself), perhaps interpreters need to attend more to cultural sensitivity (sometimes called "good attitude"), and heed special notice to the behaviors that they as a team have with Deaf people. One way in which this is accomplished is by the modality the team chooses to use for feeds, support, and negotiation. The modality the team uses reflects how they see the interaction with Deaf participants; the positioning of the team to be more visibly accessible to Deaf participants can also make the team interpreting more collectivistic and collaborative.

We have seen that interpreting teams can work collaboratively and interdependently on all aspects of the interpreting assignment and related decision-making. One important decision is how open this process is to the Deaf participants in the situation. Wilson argues that ASL signers should have access to the feeds and collaboration of the team, and in fact they should be part of the team's process. This process is illustrated in Figure 7.1, which can be contrasted to Figure 7.2 which illustrates the fact that the Deaf participants are excluded from the team's feeds and collaborating when the team uses written or spoken English for this purpose.

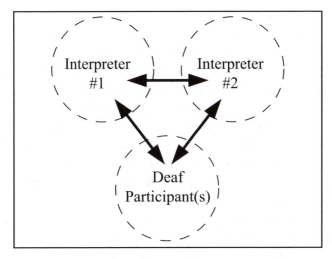

Figure 7.1. Using ASL as the Language of Collaboration and Interdependence Includes the Deaf Participant(s)

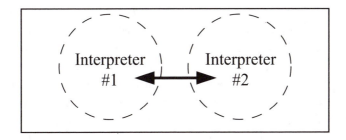

Figure 7.2. Using Written or Verbal Communication (English) as the Language of Collaboration and Interdependence Excludes the Deaf Participant(s)

Teams have a few options regarding their relationship with Deaf participants. For example, (1) they can keep their negotiations regarding their teaming work to themselves (as an independent unit); (2) they can include Deaf participants at only specific times, such as when determining placement; or (3) they can include Deaf participants throughout. Wilson's Open Process Model of team interpreting is focused on the last of these three.

Hauser, Finch, and Hauser discuss the relationship between the interpreter and the Deaf person.[7] They introduce a Deaf Professional-Designated Interpreter Model that elaborates on the ongoing working relationship and interpersonal connection between a Deaf professional (such as a psychotherapist, doctor, or film director) and a designated interpreter who works regularly with that professional. They argue the case that the interpreter should work closely with the professional and to follow the professional's lead, which is in great contrast to the Neutral Conduit Model that defines the interpreting process as something that is quite separate and apart from the Deaf person's work duties and activities. In the Deaf professional-designated interpreter relationship, the interpreter combines his or her skills as an interpreter with a growing working knowledge of the professional's field and the dynamics of the work environment, engages in ongoing negotiation regarding the interpreting role and how to best work with the professional (again, by largely following the professional's lead), and may share observations and opinions with the professional, as someone who is part of that professional's team. This relationship grows over time and requires teamwork, mutual respect, and trust on the part of both individuals. It is apparent that Figure 7.1 would also illustrate the relationship between a Deaf professional and a designated team of interpreters. The field needs to determine to what extent it wants to pursue an Open Process Model of team interpreting more broadly in the field.

Napier, Carmichael, and Wiltshire report on a case study in which they analyze the interaction between an Australian Deaf professional and a team (pair) of interpreters before, during, and after the interpretation of the Deaf professional's conference presentation.[8] They report that the Deaf professional and the two interpreters have a briefing (their term) before the presentation in which they discuss signals that they can use to make the interpretation go smoothly, and they discuss how to handle special issues. The special issues include one part of the presentation in which the Deaf professional does not want the interpreters to interpret (voice) a portion of his presentation and another part of the presentation for which the Deaf professional gives the interpreters a written copy of a quotation to read (rather than having them interpret the quotation from his signing). The Deaf professional and the two interpreters make use of pauses, nods, and eye contact to signal each other during the interpretation. In addition, one of the interpreters uses an open palm hand to indicate that he is still interpreting and the other interpreter sometimes signs, "YES," or "GOOD." The interpreters and the Deaf professional also debrief afterwards. Napier, Carmichael, and Wiltshire recommend that Deaf professionals work with the same interpreters over time if possible, that they cross over traditional interpreter boundaries by working more closely with interpreters, and that they brief interpreters, which, they propose, empowers the Deaf professional more than if there is no briefing.

The kind of teamwork between the Deaf professional and the team of interpreters, which Napier, Carmichael, and Wiltshire report, indicates that teaming extends beyond the interpreters, and needs to involve the Deaf participants. At least, this is the case for Deaf professionals. It is likely that there are many more instances in which the "boundary" between the interpreting team and the Deaf participants needs to be less pronounced, as suggested by Wilson. Sluis & De Wit, for example, state, "In our view, a team consists of all the parties involved in the assignment: consumers and interpreters."[9]

It has been many years since interpreters began to consider their unique relationship with Deaf participants, and it seems that team interpreting is in a similar position now. Namely, what is the relationship between a team of interpreters and Deaf participants? That is, what does it mean for the team–as a working unit–to be a helper, machine, communication facilitator, cultural mediator, or ally? This is an area that needs to be further explored in the field, and more research is needed in this area as well.

SURVEY RESULTS: MODALITY AND LANGUAGE PREFERENCES

The survey asked interpreters which modality and language they tend to use when communicating with a team interpreter. The survey states, "The following three questions relate to the modality and language that are used by interpreters to communicate with each other during the interpretation." For modality, respondents were asked to choose from the following options: *signed, spoken, written,* or *other.* If they checked *other,* they could write in a different response. For language, the options were *ASL, English, nonverbal communication,* or *other.* Again, they could write in a different response if they checked *other.* The survey also asked respondents to "Explain why you tend to use the above modality and language."

The most commonly selected modality was *signed,* which was selected by seventeen interpreters. Of the forty-six completed surveys, two (4.3%) of the respondents seemed confused by the question regarding modality and language. Based on their responses, it is clear that they thought this question had to do with which language they tend to interpret into the most (e.g., ASL-to-English or English-to-ASL). Therefore, these two responses were discounted and are not included here, so seventeen out of forty-four (38.6%) (valid) responses selected *signed*.

Fifteen respondents (34%) selected *other* and wrote in either *all three* or *it depends on the situation* rather than choosing from the options listed (signed, spoken, or written). Therefore, these two responses would seem to be highly indicative of the modalities that the respondents tend to use, that is, both signed and all three modalities/it depends on the situation. Also, although this question did not ask for an explanation, two-thirds of the respondents who stated either all three modalities or it depends on the situation (ten of the fifteen respondents) wrote on the survey that it depended on the particulars of the team interpreting assignment. Most of these respondents did not elaborate on the factors that would determine their choice other than to say it depended on the setting, clients, and situation. However, two interpreters did mention specific factors that determined their modality choice: (a) the logistics of the interpreters, e.g., if the interpreters were facing each other or next to each other and (b) the target language at the moment–with a preference for using the target language for feeds or, at times, to use writing regardless of the target language. In addition, one of these respondents reported usually using signed and written modalities the most, and another reported using the signed modality the most although they both stated that the modality they use depends on the context. These two responses were coded as all three modalities/it depends on the situation for the purposes of this study.

Written and spoken modalities were clearly selected the least (with six respondents, 13.6%; and five respondents, 11.4%, respectively). In addition, one interpreter responded that both signed and written were what s/he tended to use (one respondent; 2%). See Figure 7.3.

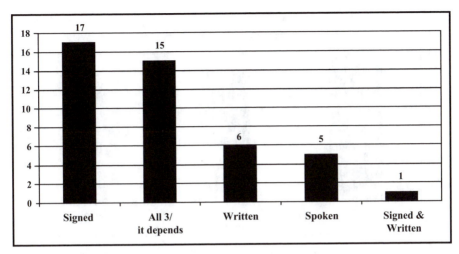

Figure 7.3. Preferred modality (signed, written, or spoken)

The interpreters' language choice corresponds to their responses to the modality question. Seventeen of the forty-four respondents (38.6%) chose ASL as the language they tend to use, which is exactly the same number as those who chose *signed* as the modality they tend to use (again discounting two responses). The second and third choices were very close. Fourteen respondents (31.8%) selected English and thirteen respondents (29.5%) stated they tended to use *a mix of the three language options* or that *it depends on the situation*. Respondents did not elaborate on their reasons for tending to use particular languages other than to say it depends on the needs of the moment and what they deem to be most appropriate at that particular time; however, a couple of respondents commented that it depends on the needs of the team interpreter, and whether the team is conferring or interpreting. No one chose the *nonverbal communication* option, but one person stated a tendency to use all the language options, but went on to state that s/he uses nonverbal communication more than the others. (This person's response was coded as *a mix of the three language options*.) See Figure 7.4.

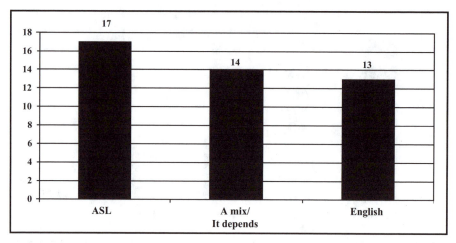

Figure 7.4. Preferred language use (ASL, English, or nonverbal communication)

The next question on the survey asked interpreters to respond to the following: "Explain why you tend to use the above modality and language." The responses to this question provide some insight into why some interpreters tend to use a certain modality/language and what is involved in the decision-making of interpreters regarding how they select which modality and language to use at any given time. As we review their responses, we will focus on *when* these modalities/languages are used and *why* they are used at those times. In addition, we will review some pros and cons of the modality/language options as provided by the respondents.

Most of the interpreters in the survey reported that they tend to use ASL when communicating with a team interpreter; most of these respondents stated that they preferred to use ASL both when communicating with the other interpreter during the interpreting process and when providing an information feed. Some interpreters stated that they would use ASL if the interpreters were facing each other or if they were farther away (because it would be easier to communicate using the visual language), and one interpreter stated having a tendency to use ASL when processing before and after with a Deaf interpreter. However, many of these interpreters also stated that they often use spoken English to feed information when the target language is English.

The most cited reasons for using ASL include the following: (a) an ASL feed is the least disruptive to the hearing people present and does not draw too much attention to the feed, (b) the use of ASL provides equal access for Deaf people which enables them to know what is going on seamlessly, and (c) using ASL in the presence of Deaf people is the most respectful and helps to build trust. One interpreter also mentioned that ASL feeds are good to use in a situation where the interpreters cannot speak out loud, and several interpreters mentioned that it was the most natural and useful way to provide a feed. Conversely, some interpreters who said that they do not tend to use ASL stated that it could be distracting, and a couple of the interpreters who tend to use ASL said the type of setting needs to be factored into the decision whether or not to use ASL; and, again, some mentioned that although they generally use ASL, they preferred to provide an information feed in English when the target language is English.

The high number of those who chose *signed/ASL* as the modality and language they tend to use for feeds and collaborating may surprise some readers. We should note here that the survey did not ask if interpreters interpret more from ASL to English or from English to ASL. Given the fact that many situations involve interpretation from English to ASL because Deaf people are in the minority and interpreting services are often provided for access to events in the majority culture, it is likely that interpreters tend to interpret more into ASL than they interpret into English. Also, since a *mixture of ASL* and *English* or *it depends* were not options in the survey and yet a large number wrote in these two comments, these responses indicate that much depends on the situation. It is particularly evident in interpreters' comments that they tend to prefer to feed each other using the TL.

The majority of the respondents said that they tend to use whispered English when the target language is English even if they generally use ASL. Several also mentioned that they use English when processing their work before and after the interpreting assignment, and when providing feedback to each other. Some mentioned that they use English when they are sitting close to each other (so the communication could happen easily and would not be distracting). The most common reason given for providing an information feed in English was that it is more efficient when the target language is English; some of these interpreters also mentioned that visual feeds may be less effective when voicing. One interpreter, for instance, explained that it is easier for the lead interpreter to incorporate the information into the target language when it is fed in the target language and that the interpreter may actually just copy what was fed and use that. One interpreter stated a preference for getting information feeds in English (this interpreter's native language), and stated that it was more difficult to manage getting feeds in ASL and to keep up with the information. On the other hand, a few interpreters (who did not select *spoken/English*) mentioned that providing a feed in English can be disruptive or rude.

Although respondents who said that they tend to use all of the modality/ language options generally stated that their choice of modality/language depends on the situation and the preference of the other team interpreter, most of these respondents stated that they tend to provide a feed in the target language. At the same time, many of these respondents also stated that they would check with the team interpreter to see how they best receive a feed. Overall, however, these interpreters stress the fact that interpreters work in a variety of places and in a variety of situations, so there is no one-size-fits-all approach when it comes to determining the modality and language to use at a particular time. What is key is to be flexible and to adjust to the particular partner and situation–using written notes, English, and ASL, depending on what would be most effective at the moment. Some stated that the choice depends on the kind of information to be fed, the set up (where the interpreters and participants are located in the room), the urgency of the feed or communication, and perhaps confidentiality (not having the feed accessible due to reasons of confidentiality).

Interpreters who mentioned using written communication commented on two reasons for using the written form: (a) to write notes during the interpretation for later discussion of information or feedback, and (b) to write information feeds. Most commonly, written statements were confined to comments, suggestions, and questions; and a couple of respondents stated that they would use a written feed only if the feed did not need to be incorporated quickly. Some respondents stated that written feeds are the least obtrusive, but an equal number of respondents stated that written communication could be construed as rude and, therefore, they preferred not to use written feeds. One interpreter commented that using written English was nice for the lead interpreter because this interpreter could choose to look or not, and did not have to cognitively stop processing in order to pick up the teammate's signed or spoken communication. Another interpreter commented that a written feed can cause the lead interpreter to lose track of the message. However, other interpreters stated that the lead interpreter could read the note after changing to the monitor interpreter role, and that was a benefit for the team; and one person stated that it provided a mental break to read English. Finally, one interpreter commented that s/he always shreds the notes at home to protect people's privacy.

Respondents mentioned very little about nonverbal communication in the survey, but some respondents did say that nonverbal communication can best be used when the interpreters can see each other well. These interpreters mentioned that nonverbal communication can be used to provide a hint or cue for the lead interpreter, and can be used to provide feedback or affirmations regarding the lead interpreter's interpretation. One interpreter stated that nonverbal communication can be useful if the team interpreters plan for this ahead of time, but that nonverbal communication can be misinterpreted if it not used often and consistently. Likewise, another interpreter mentioned that nonverbal communication works best when team members know each other well. One interpreter explained how s/he uses nonverbal communication by stating, "I nod when I love the sign/word choice. When I know the interpreter, I pat them on the back and whisper good job as we switch."

One interpreter's comments stand in contrast to the comments provided by the other interpreters on modality/language choice. This interpreter wrote:

> I am increasingly more interested in having my team just take the interpretation if I don't "have it." The passing of the work back and forth can be seamless and complete if both interpreters are working in synch. This eliminates the need to vocalize or sign "feeds" which the "on" interpreter is often unable to incorporate into the interpretation.

This approach involves a more fluid give and take in the actual production of the target language, and would negate the need for information feeds. The question still remains, however, when this approach is best used and when feeding information (whether by using ASL, whispered English, written English, or nonverbal communication) may provide a better option. The question is when are feed strategies more effective and when are other teaming strategies (such as *switching roles*) more effective? This is certainly an area that interpreters who work in teams would benefit from exploring further and one that will require additional research.

THOUGHT QUESTIONS 7.3
Further exploring modality and language usage
CHAPTER REVIEW AND APPLICATION

1) Do you mostly interpret into English or into ASL? Does that fact affect what modality and language you tend to use for communicating with the other interpreter during team interpreting? Explain.

2) Which do you tend to use more often: information feeds or switch roles? Why? What are the benefits and drawbacks of each of these strategies?

3) When an interpreting team uses ASL for feeds and collaboration, the Deaf participant(s) have access to (and may participate in) the interaction, and when the team uses written or spoken English for feeds and collaboration, the Deaf participant(s) are closed off to this communication. Discuss this fact with other interpreters and with Deaf people; and after exploring this more with others, explain *when* you would use ASL and when you would use (written or spoken) English, based on these discussions.

ENDNOTES

[1]   Cokely & Hawkins, 2003. Also see Cokely & Hawkins for more information regarding the use of nonverbal communication in team interpreting.

[2]   Kinsella, 1997.

[3]   M. Wilson, personal communication, January 14, 2008; also, see Richards, 2008.

[4]   Mindess, 2006.

[5]   Hoza, 2003, p. 33.

[6]   Bienvenu, 1989, p. 111.

[7]   Hauser, Finch, & Hauser, 2008.

[8]   Napier, Carmichael, & Wiltshire, 2008.

[9]   Sluis & De Wit, 2007, p. 12

CHAPTER 8

DIFFERENT TEAMS, DIFFERENT WORKING STYLES

*Build for your team a feeling of oneness,
of dependence on one another
and of strength to be derived by unity.*
—Vince Lombardi

Teams have different options for how they work together. Given that each team is unique because of the particular personal and professional relationship of the interpreters involved, their experience with working together, their philosophies of interpreting, and their approach to the team interpreting task, it follows that how they function as a team would vary depending on the composition and needs of the team. In addition, certain needs of the team become more central to their working relationship during certain interpreting assignments, or due to the specific factors of the situation or individual interpreter needs.

THOUGHT QUESTIONS 8.1
How teams work differently

1) Think of two very different interpreters with whom you team interpret, and describe how you work differently with each of them.

2) What aspects of working as a team should be consistent regardless of who the interpreters are? Explain.

3) What aspects of working as a team are the most dependent on who the team members are? Explain.

THE VIDEOTAPE STUDY: HOW THE INTERPRETING TEAMS WORKED DIFFERENTLY

All three teams employed a variety of teaming strategies and accomplished a successful interpretation. At the same time, the three teams worked differently in some respects.

One way in which team #1 differed from the other teams is that one of the interpreters on the team (interpreter #2) was more dependent on the other interpreter for assistance; she received 80% of the support and she offered 20% of the support. See Table 8.1. This discrepancy is evident in all five areas of support: confirmations, target language (TL) feeds (i.e., corrections and enhancements), process feeds, collaboration, and switching roles. Although the number of confirmations in Table 8.1 is the same for each interpreter, interpreter #1 actually does more nodding throughout the interpretation than interpreter #2. These two interpreters had known each other and had worked together the longest of all the teams, but they each report in the follow-up interviews that they had not teamed together for some time. Both team members also mentioned in the interviews that they felt they each had different needs, and that they felt they worked well together and provided what they each needed overall.

Note that only verbal confirmations or nodding in response to a request for confirmation (or in response to a solicitous look) are counted as confirmations in this study. There are many instances in which the monitor interpreter continues to nod when the lead interpreter is interpreting; however, this act is difficult to quantify because it occurs often and sometimes continues for more than a minute at a time. This kind of continuous nodding is not included in this figure.

Strategy	This team's total strategies	Interpreter #1's strategies	Interpreter #2's strategies
TL feed	9[1]	8	1
Confirmation	6	3 (more nodding)	3 (some nodding)
Process feed	10	8	2
Collaboration	8	7	1
Switch roles	2	2	0
TOTAL	35	28	7
Total %	100%	80%	20%

Table 8.1. Total number of strategies for interpreting team #1.

Interpreter #1 also changed the timing of the support she offered during this interpretation. When she was in the monitor role during the first part of the interpretation, she would wait 2 to 4 seconds before offering an information feed (in the form of either a TL feed or a process feed). However, there is a notable change 10 minutes into the 42-minute interpretation, at which point she collaborates with interpreter #2 by telling her, "Wait a second" (i.e., to wait longer before producing the TL rendition). After this point, interpreter #1 waits from 6 to 8 seconds before offering an information feed. This change in timing of the teaming strategies allowed for interpreter #2 to have more process time, and even though she paused or hesitated at times, interpreter #2 would more often get the meaning across without a feed, although there were still instances in which interpreter #1 would provide an information feed. In contrast, interpreter #2 often would wait 6 to 8 seconds throughout the interpretation before offering support by way of a feed to interpreter #1. It may well be that if interpreter #1 had waited longer to feed throughout the interpretation, it is possible that there would have been fewer feeds in this interpretation.

The fact that one interpreter provided most of the feeds and the fact that interpreter #1 altered the timing of her support by allowing interpreter #2 additional process time highlights two features of team interpreting. First, the needs of teams vary. It could be that in a given interpretation, both interpreters will need a comparable number of feeds and support, or it could be that one interpreter may be more dependent upon the other team interpreter due to the content or context, due to unfamiliarity with the situation, or due to comparative lack of skill. Second, team members may adapt to each other's needs during the experience of teaming together, as when becoming accustomed to each other's process time and becoming more aware of the other interpreter's need for particular kinds of support.

Team #2 is the only team that neither made any corrections nor switched roles. This team also offered the most confirmations of the three teams. This support was explicitly stated in seventeen instances with such expressions as "Nice" or "Very nice," and twelve of these instances occurred at the completion of an interpreting turn. The other five occurred after the monitor interpreter acknowledged the word choice or phrasing choice of the lead interpreter, as when the lead interpreter said, "It's almost like they're becoming surrogate mothers" and "You're pulling teeth sometimes trying to..." These explicit confirmations account for most of the strategies used in this team's interpretation, and neither of the other two teams used such explicit expressions (such as "Nice"). During the follow-up interviews, both interpreters stated that they appreciated getting this kind of support from the other interpreter because they were nervous about the task, and they both said they wanted to reciprocate in kind.

The fact that these interpreters did not offer corrections or use the switch roles strategy actually shows how they approached their team interpreting work for the interpretation. Both interpreters stated during their interviews that they did not want to interfere with their team member's interpreting process, so they tended to not feed information. Likewise, both interpreters stated that they would only switch roles if requested to do so, or if they had gotten permission to do so from the team interpreter before beginning the interpretation. This is the only team that seemed hesitant to engage in these two teaming strategies during the interpretation (switching roles and correcting). This team also had the least amount of experience with both interpreting and team interpreting. This could account for their reluctance. Both of these interpreters stated in the follow-up interviews that they personally find it more difficult to process information that is being provided by the monitor interpreter (as with corrections), i.e., they struggle with the extra cognitive load associated with processing information feeds.[2]

Both team members actually do provide some information feeds and these are given when the lead interpreter is obviously struggling, as when taking a long process time or when hesitating (e.g., when the signer is fingerspelling in the SL and the interpreter is trying to figure out what was fingerspelled). So, at least in these instances, the interpreters were comfortable providing support in the form of a *process feed* during the interpretation. Predominantly, however, confirmations were the primary strategy used by these interpreters in their teaming work.

Team #3 functioned differently from the other teams in two primary ways. First, this team approached the warm-up video differently and their subsequent discussion differed as well. This difference carried through the entire interpretation. Team #3 was the only team to voice the warm-up video to help them prepare for the interpretation. Doing so allowed them to discuss–in the pre-session–this experience of having voiced for these panelists. Their discussion of their goals was more explicit and specific than those of the other two teams, in that these two interpreters discussed specific cultural adjustments that they may want to make in the interpretation. These included concepts that would be unfamiliar to the TL audience, cultural nuance that may be important to convey (such as using "we" to express the panelists' shared cultural experiences), expressing the rapport between the moderator and the panelists, and using customary forms of address (e.g., using the moderator's first name when addressing her). In particular, they discussed actual wording (phrases and sentences) that they could use in the TL rendition. The team wrote down key words (such as *culture* and *we*) on paper, referred to these terms occasionally during the interpretation (to keep these concepts in mind) and used some of this wording in the interpretation to provide a more coherent and culturally equivalent interpretation, and the support they provided each other during the interpretation also focused largely on these particular aspects of meaning in the interpretation. They also wrote the following, in order to keep them in mind during the interpretation: *affect* and *register*.

Second, whereas this team uses all of the strategies except corrections to support the team's work, almost all of these appear in the written form. Neither of the other teams use written communications for the purpose of supporting, or feeding, the team. In the follow-up interviews, the interpreters in team #3 explained that they tend to write down notes either for themselves for later reference or for the team member. They also stated that if they want to share a brief note with the other interpreter, they do so when they switch roles. However, if the note is intended for immediate use by the lead interpreter, the interpreter in the monitor role signals for the lead interpreter to read the note (generally by holding up the sheet of paper to inside the lead interpreter's line of vision). Both interpreters were quite comfortable with this process and spoke highly of it, and they both seemed a bit surprised when they were told that the other two teams did not use written notes during their interpretations.

Team #3 used half the number of strategies of the other two teams (fifteen total for team #3, as compared to thirty-five for team #1 and thirty-two for team #2). See Table 8.2. In addition, a little over half of these were confirmations (53%, which is the same percentage as for team #2), and team #3 also offers no corrections.[3] The members of this team reported that they often work together as a team and have been diligently working on how they can best team together. See Figure 8.1 for the totals of all the teaming strategies used by the three teams represented as a pie chart. (All percentages on Table 8.2 and Figure 8.1 are rounded to the nearest whole percentage point.)

Strategy	*Team #1*		*Team #2*		*Team #3*		*TOTAL*	
TL feed	9	*26%*	0	*0%*	1	*7%*	10[4]	*12%*
Confirmation	6	*17%*	17	*53%*	8	*53%*	31	*38%*
Process feed	10	*29%*	7	*22%*	2	*13%*	19	*23%*
Collaboration	8	*23%*	8	*25%*	3	*20%*	19	*23%*
Switch roles	2	*6%*	0	*0%*	1	*7%*	3	*4%*
TOTAL	*35*		*32*		*15*		*82*	

Table 8.2. Teaming strategies used by the three teams.[5]

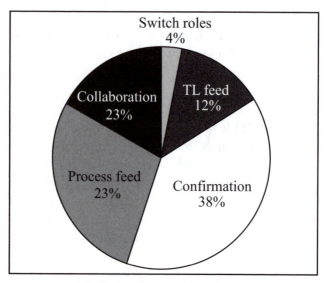

Figure 8.1. Strategies used by the three teams

Not all interpreting teams work the same way. As we see with team #1, team members may differ in both the number and the kinds of support they provide each other, as well as alter their approaches depending on the needs of the team and the other interpreter's process time. With team #2, we see that how much moral support is offered varies and is dependent on the team members and their sense of each other's need for emotional support, and we see that both corrections and the changing role strategy are dependent on the team's mutual agreement that these are options that can help the team. With team #3, we see that having mutually shared goals about what the interpretation should look like can help the interpretation, and we see that if a team uses written feeds, the team must have a system for handling the sharing of information in the notes (as was the case with this team).

DISCUSSION: HOW THE INTERPRETING TEAMS WORKED DIFFERENTLY (OPTIONS FOR HOW TEAMS CAN WORK TOGETHER)

Ideally, interpreters become a single functioning unit when they work as a team, and, as such, the team members determine how to best work together and to support the work of the team. Processing the team interpreting afterwards, as was mentioned in the follow-up interviews, serves the team by allowing them to determine what is working for them and what they may need to alter the next time they team together. It also provides the team with a sense of commitment to each other.

We have seen that one interpreter in team #1 provided most of the feeds and that this interpreter delayed feeds by allowing the lead interpreter more process time, and both of these approaches met the needs of the team. It must be noted that there is a certain amount of inequity of skills in any team, but an issue could arise if one interpreter truly is not capable of handling the interpreting work. If an interpreter is not ready to team in that setting, then the team may not be able to function as a real team that is both collaborative and interdependent. This must be a consideration in situations in which the team is made up of a novice and a mentor, whose skills differ greatly. While the mentor is providing mentorship to the novice, the degree to which they can truly function as a team may be limited. Successful *interdependence* is based on the foundation of the ability of each member to work *independently*, so that working with someone else provides additional resources for success. It is important when a novice and a mentor interpret together that they are comfortable with the inequity of their ability to contribute to the interpreting work.

Team #2 was reluctant to provide corrections or to switch roles, but the team was very comfortable using confirmations, as well as process feeds and collaboration. It seems that teams need to figure out how they can best make corrections and how they want to go about switching roles, as needed, so that both of these strategies can benefit the team's work. In addition, confirmations are valued and, at times, extremely necessary to maintain the confidence of the team. At the same time, expressions such as "Nice" and "That was very good," which seem more like affirmations (and were only used by this team), may be perceived as empty praise. There are two possible issues with using confirmations to the extreme. First, these types of confirmations can begin to sound empty, or can begin to cause the lead interpreter to wonder about the lack of support at those times when such support is not given (e.g., they may think, "They haven't said, 'Nice.' That's right. I'm not doing as well now"). Second, if the team's primary means of support is these types of confirmations at the expense of other teaming strategies (such as corrections and switching roles), there may be an issue with meeting the team's needs.

Team #3 shared common goals in terms of what they wanted to convey in the TL and most of their communication during the interpretation appeared in the written form. Sharing goals seems to represent an effort to be explicit about what the team is trying to accomplish and ensures that they are sharing a common schema and goal for this interpretation. It represents an effort to collaborate and to be interdependent throughout their time together as a team. As far as using the written form, the choice of modality (visual or auditory) and language (ASL or English) needs to be consciously determined by the team, and needs to be reassessed occasionally (or altered depending on the context). Written notes for voicing may be an approach that teams have not considered and may be worth pursuing–although it is more individualistic. At the same time, the use of ASL to communicate during the interpretation–to include Deaf participants in the teaming process–provides a more collectivistic approach to teaming.

Regardless of how each team works, the need for commitment and trust is paramount. Covey (the author of the acclaimed book *The Seven Habits of Highly Effective People*) provides guidance on how to build trust and increase interdependence by using the analogy of making deposits into an emotional bank account.[6] "Courtesy, kindness, honesty, and keeping…commitments" comprise the deposits, and trust increases as this connection and sense of safety is enhanced over time.[7] People feel safer with others who have made sufficient and consistent deposits into the emotional bank account. Covey proposes six major kinds of deposits, which are essentially interpersonal features that support interdependence. These six kinds of major deposits are listed here with a summary of the definitions from Covey, and the list includes information on what each feature means for team interpreting.

SIX MAJOR DEPOSITS (adapted from Covey):[8]

1) Understanding the individual
<u>Definition:</u> committing oneself to the value of the person and what is important to the person
<u>For team interpreting, this means:</u> appreciating the other team member as a person and as an interpreter, as well as learning and keeping in mind what is important to that person in terms of his or her needs, goals, and desires as an individual and as a team member.

2) Attending to the little things
Definition: little acts of kindness and courtesy, and showing respect
For team interpreting, this means: being kind, courteous, and respectful; maintaining a rapport that is both positive and supportive.

3) Keeping commitments
Definition: keeping promises and maintaining trustworthiness
For team interpreting, this means: following through with strategies that you agree to use, and continuing to commit to make the team interpreting work.

4) Clarifying expectations
Definition: working at arriving at mutually agreeable expectations
For team interpreting, this means: making an ongoing effort to clarify expectations for each person that can benefit the team; these can include ways of signaling support, ways of offering support, ways to handle situations that arise, ways to process what happens, and to make changes, etc.

5) Showing personal integrity
Definition: being honest, and "keeping promises and fulfilling expectations"
For team interpreting, this means: being truthful about what you can and cannot offer, as well as how you work as a team, and following through with commitments to the team and expectations as mutually agreed upon.

6) Apologizing sincerely when you make a withdrawal
Definition: honestly saying you are sorry about mistakes
For team interpreting, this means: owning and apologizing for any errors in judgment or any violations of any of the 'deposits'/interpersonal features that support interdependence.

THOUGHT QUESTIONS 8.2
Thinking about how teams work differently

1) The three teams in the videotape study differed in how they worked as a team. What aspects of these teams' work are you most likely to incorporate into your own teaming work? Explain.

2) What aspects of these teams' work are you most likely not to incorporate into your own teaming work? Explain.

3) Discuss with an interpreter how these three teams functioned differently, and highlight what you get out of that discussion.

SURVEY RESULTS: HOW TEAMS MAY FUNCTION DIFFERENTLY

Twenty-seven of the forty-six respondents (58.7%) answered one of the final survey questions that was optional. This question asked interpreters to respond to the following: "Teams may function differently (work with each other differently) depending on the interpreters and the particular context. Please give an example or two of how teams may function differently. (optional)" Because the three teams in the videotape study varied considerably in how they worked together, the purpose of this question was to try to ascertain the kinds of variables that may alter the way interpreters work as a team.

The most common response to this question was "it depends." Fourteen respondents out of the twenty-seven respondents (51.9%) stated that the specifics of the situation are important in determining how a team may function differently. These interpreters discussed both the types of teams and the types of situations as important factors.

These respondents mentioned a variety of types of teams as a variable. These include the following: a hearing interpreter/Deaf interpreter team; a team with a spoken language interpreter; a staff interpreter/freelance interpreter team, in which the staff interpreter is more familiar with the setting and takes on more of a lead role because the freelance interpreter is new to the situation; and a mentor/protégé relationship, in which the mentor would take on more of a responsibility for the interpreting work and for providing feedback to the protégé.

Specific settings mentioned include the following: a workshop in which the team may function "almost as one," a theater production in which the team will interpret predetermined characters, the legal setting which has its own prescribed operating procedures, a VRS (video relay service) setting which may require more voicing feeds vs. a workshop or class which may focus more on switching and less on feeds, interpreting an event that is taking place outside as opposed to inside (with more interaction possible in the outside setting, generally speaking), and interpreting a working luncheon in which one interpreter eats while the other interprets (and they switch back and forth in spurts). It seems that one interpreter in particular may have captured the sentiment of many when writing the following:

This, of course, is a loaded question in that how a team works will depend on a number of things about the interpreters: each of their skill levels, previous work experience, personalities, prior experience working together, etc. On top of that is the setting, the consumers both deaf and hearing, as well as the topic. To make a "clean" setting, let's say you have a meeting with 5 signers and 5 non-signers. In one instance, say the two interpreters assigned have never met, one is very familiar with the meeting, [and] the other is not. Assume that both are pretty balanced skill-wise and both have similar amounts and types of interpreting experience. The experienced person can tell the co[-interpreter] as much as he or she knows and also start the meeting. The experienced person may voice all deaf people for the first 15 minutes or so until the new person gets a sense of each person's signing style. Now take the same situation and put in two interpreters who are both familiar with the meeting and each other. There may need to be very little information sharing, discussing, or feeding. Again with the same situation, say the familiar interpreter is highly skilled and the new interpreter is not. But say that this interpreter is also very experienced and does not realize his or her own weaknesses. The familiar interpreter will have to be very cautious in how he or she says things to the other interpreter, including how often he or she gives feeds and for what.

Five of the twenty-seven respondents (18.5%) focused on how teams may differ in how they make use of feeds and feedback. Two interpreters commented that it is best to put together interpreters for teaming who agree on whether or not they want to use feeds during an assignment and want to provide feedback afterwards. One commented that it seems that graduates of interpreting programs, those who have more confidence in their own skills, and those who can separate the work from their own identity are more likely to want to receive feedback and discuss their interpreting work. Two interpreters commented that sometimes a team interpreter may feed too much due to the fact that the other interpreter has a longer processing time, so may feed unnecessarily and may not adequately monitor the other interpreter's process time.

Five interpreters (18.5%) stated that interpreters may divide up tasks differently depending on the interpreters' skills and the particulars of the situation. These interpreters offered several options. Two respondents stated that interpreters may divide up the interpreting based on the target language, with one interpreter doing all of the voicing (ASL-to-English interpreting) and the other doing all of the signing (English-to-ASL interpreting), and this determination is based on comfort level with each language and whether or not the interpreter is a native user of the language (e.g., a child of Deaf adults [coda]). Two interpreters mentioned that interpreters may alternate interpreting for the participants in a highly interactive environment, i.e., each interpreter will interpret for every other speaker. Also, one respondent stated that dividing up the task in this way was sometimes more efficient depending on the set-up of the room, e.g., if the interpreters had to be across the room from each other. This respondent also stated that it was important to get input from consumers regarding what would work best, and that the interpreters need to strategize together to determine the best possible placement and how to split the responsibility of interpreting based on the specifics of the interpreting context. Last, one interpreter said that interpreters sometimes divide up the tasks with one interpreter doing the actual interpreting work and the other interpreter taking care of logistics.

Three interpreters (11.1%) focused on the fact that feeds sometimes differed, depending on the team. Specifically, one interpreter commented that some interpreters want the missed concept, while others want a word or two. Another interpreter stated that some prefer a feed in English and others prefer a feed in ASL, depending if that interpreter wants to just "copy sign" in order to keep going when the target language is ASL or if the text is a frozen text, such as a song. The other interpreter who commented on varying the kinds of feeds stated that the feed can consist of one interpreter "taking over" the interpretation, the interpreter may also lean in to indicate a readiness to feed, or the interpreter could wait to see if the lead interpreter needs some additional process time to continue interpreting.

Three other topics were also mentioned in response to this question. Two interpreters (7.4%) stated that how well the interpreters know each other and trust each other affects how willing they are to accept feeds and to openly discuss what is or is not working. One put it this way: "If you don't know each other, you won't know their skill level, style, strengths, weaknesses. That is different than a person you work with regularly and have established [an] unspoken way of approaching the work." One interpreter mentioned that the team may or may not stick to switching off every 30 minutes, and may in fact switch off after 20 minutes if that provides for a better natural break (e.g., if a speaker is done after 20 minutes), so it is best that the team not make a big deal out of the division of time being perfectly equitable at these times. One interpreter mentioned the fact that an interpreting team may use an "open process," and this alters how the team functions; this interpreter described an open process as the following:

> Use of the "open process" approach which, briefly, means a cue is not given to the interpreter but rather the needed information is simply interpreted by the "off" interpreter as part of the interpretation and then the "on" interpreter continues with the work.

The type of team and the type of setting may affect how the team works together. Also, other factors include how the tasks are divided up based on the interpreters' skills or the setting, whether or not the team uses feeds (or other teaming strategies) or feedback, how information feeds and other communication occur, whether or not an open process is used, how well the team knows each other, and the timing of shifts. All these factors play an important role in determining how the interpreters can best function as a team.

THOUGHT QUESTIONS 8.3
Further exploring how teams work differently
CHAPTER REVIEW AND APPLICATION

1) First, look back at the last few times you have team interpreted and write down the variables that altered how you worked as a team. Second, discuss these variables with another interpreter and write your thoughts about how these variables affect how the team works together.

2) Discuss how teams determine who will take the lead role in a particular setting. Identify key factors that determine this decision.

3) When is an open teaming process usually employed and when is a closed teaming process usually employed? What factors determine when a team uses each of these?

ENDNOTES

[1] Corrections account for two-thirds of the TL feeds used by team #1 (i.e., six corrections); the other one-third of the TL feeds (three), of course, were enhancements.

[2] Two other reasons a team may not be comfortable with information feeds or other teaming strategies may be that they are reluctant to step out of a more rigid interpreting role or that they do not want to risk "stepping on the other person's toes."

[3] Even though team #3 and team #2 used the same percentage of confirmations, the confirmations used by team #3 primarily consisted of head nods; team #2 primarily used expressions such as "Nice" and "Very nice."

[4] Corrections account for six of the TL feeds used by all three teams, and of the remaining TL feeds, team #1 used three enhancements and team #3 used one.

[5] Note that because these numbers are rounded off to the nearest whole number, the total for team #1 comes out to 101%.

[6] Covey, 2004.

[7] Covey, 2004, p. 188.

[8] Covey, 2004, pp. 190-199.

CHAPTER 9

ACHIEVING AND MAINTAINING COLLABORATION AND INTERDEPENDENCE

Trust [people] and they will trust you;
treat them greatly,
and they will show themselves great.
—Ralph Waldo Emerson

Teams of interpreters can work in various ways. Two interpreters can work independently, taking turns doing the interpreting work; they can work in such a way that they alternate taking on the role of monitor interpreter in order to keep the other interpreter's process and production of the target language (TL) on track; or they can work collaboratively and interdependently on all aspects of the interpretation. This last approach has been the focus of this book. The following analogy exemplifies how a team can work collaboratively and interdependently.

AN ANALOGY

Team interpreters are like mountain climbers who are going to scale the sheer face of a peak. A team of mountain climbers needs to carefully consider who has the skills, knowledge, and ability to complete the task. The team also must know each other well, commit to the team, trust in each other, and prepare in a variety of ways. They need to be physically and psychologically prepared, have all their equipment ready, and make sure the equipment is of good quality. They must also have a well thought out plan. A wrong turn can be disastrous.

These elements are fundamental to the climb. The selection of team members, the climbers' preparation, the gear, and a careful plan for the expedition are all prerequisites for a successful climb.

All of these elements continue to be important throughout the climb. However, the ascent itself is more dynamic and immediate. The climbers, the gear, and the mountain interact in predictable and surprising ways. The climbers are tested; they need to use their physical strength and their intellect. They have to take risks, pay attention, think critically, and work together as they complete each leg of the journey up the mountainside. The equipment is tested and must pass muster, or the team may make modifications as needed. The team constantly monitors the climb and is flexible and yet careful in its adjustments. The mountain is the only real constant, but it is also a moving target. It has its own contour and the team learns to adjust and adapt to its form and its special challenges: a sheer face here, an outcropping there. All of the members are capable, but they also need to assist each other and work together at various points in the journey upward.

Although the success of a single person is possible, a team has the greatest potential for success, especially when the going gets tough. Arriving at the summit is the final goal, and the satisfaction of success is palpable. The team makes it to the top by pulling together its strengths and by working as a unit with each person contributing in various ways. This is the nature of collaboration and interdependence. It involves a common goal, a common commitment, and depending on oneself as well as others to achieve the objective. Individuals buoy each other and form a cohesive unit which is stronger than each of its parts.

Collaboration and interdependence are the key components of an effective team of interpreters, just as it is for a team of mountain climbers. The important practical question is, How can collaboration and interdependence be achieved for a team of interpreters? The two studies provide the first step in clarifying the answer to this question.

For the remainder of this chapter, we review two more topics concerning achieving and maintaining collaboration and interdependence. First, we explore the nature of change and what that means for interpreters who are beginning to work under this new paradigm. Second, we identify three potential barriers that need to be better understood in order to achieve and maintain collaboration and interdependence as a team of interpreters.

THOUGHT QUESTIONS 9.1
Achieving collaboration and interdependence

1) Given that collaboration and interdependence between team members are at the foundation of effective team interpreting, what barriers exist that can impede achieving collaboration and interdependence?

2) In what ways can interpreters break down these barriers to collaboration and interdependence in teaming?

3) Choose a metaphor or analogy for team interpreting (other than comparing it to mountain climbers), explain how this metaphor or analogy works, and explain why you chose this metaphor/analogy.

WORKING THROUGH CHANGE

We have explored the notions of collaboration and interdependence in depth; the natural next question is, How can a team achieve and maintain collaboration and interdependence? When a new paradigm emerges in a field–as is the case with the collaborative and interdependent view of teaming–we must remember that practitioners are "reminiscent of their roots." This fact needs to be understood in order for teams to achieve the new paradigm.

Although the interpreting field began with an independent view of team interpreting, the field progressed to a monitoring view of teaming, which can be described as an "independent, but–" view, in that the "feed" interpreter lets the "on" interpreter do his/her interpreting work except to make a correction or to confirm that the interpretation is accurate. The field is now ushering in a collaborative and interdependent view of teaming, which is similar to what Walker calls a "we" mentality of teaming, in which interpreters see themselves as "co-interpreting" rather than simply "co-working" (simply working together).[1] There is a real sense of synergy between the interpreters that contributes to the overall effectiveness of the interpreting task for which they share responsibility. During the interpretation, for example, it is as though the monitor interpreter is saying, "Yes! and–", as opposed to "Yes, but–."[2]

Both the independent view and the monitoring ("independent, but–") view of team interpreting carry with them some baggage that interpreters need to acknowledge and work through. Interpreters who are accustomed to an independent view of teaming have developed strategies for getting through the interpretation without any assistance and may be resistant to working cooperatively with another interpreter due to their own sense of what it means to be a skilled interpreter. They may think, "I am a competent professional and can do this on my own." There are likely few interpreters coming from this perspective, since the independent view of interpreting accounts for only 6% of the comments about teaming in the survey. However, we need to recognize that these interpreters are dealing with a major shift in paradigm that involves the way in which they work as an interpreter, as well as their assumptions about interpreting and the strategies that can work for them as part of a team. They also need to have the experience with teaming that shows them that it is worthwhile to change.

Interpreters who are used to the monitoring ("independent, but–") approach to interpreting may have focused on correcting each other but little else, so they may find the transition to the "we" approach difficult for different reasons. While many interpreters may have experienced the kinds of interactions and support with a team interpreter that have gone beyond a strictly "feed" interpreter/"on" interpreter approach, there are many who have been functioning within this view for a long time. This is not to say that they cannot make the adjustment, but rather that they may feel a sense of being damaged as a result of the constant corrections during their interpreting work or the critiques offered to them afterwards as feedback. The "we" approach cannot be achieved if there is a focus on critique of each individual interpreter's work because this dynamic does not establish the cooperative and open relationship that is needed for true collaboration and interdependence. The monitoring ("independent, but–") approach is based on one-upmanship, with each interpreter taking on the role of the "evaluator." This dynamic may have been further reinforced by an interpreter's training either within an interpreting program or in the workshops one has taken, where the focus may be on "correcting" what interpreters are doing.

Interpreters who are accustomed to the "independent, but–" approach to teaming may not trust that a true collaboration can result (the monitoring view accounts for 62% of the comments about team interpreting in the survey). Their sense of what team interpreting is and the strategies they have developed may seem out of place in this new paradigm. Actually, many of these strategies can be quite useful, e.g., the establishment of various kinds of signals, and how to feed and communicate during the interpretation. What needs to be explored more is how to better talk about the team interpreting work and to recognize that taking an evaluative stance can actually work against the team. Interpreters do not want to feel that they are being evaluated every time they work in a team. So, how the interpreters work together and discuss the work needs to be examined. For example, when someone says something like, "Not to be critical, but–," we all know that a critique is coming. In the next section of this chapter, we will explore how teams can talk about their work.

Given that our field is in this transition, it is important that we acknowledge this history and work through the changes. The benefits in terms of effective teams will be worth the effort. So how *do* interpreting teams change their assumptions and strategies, or develop new ones that can help them achieve a sense of "we"?

THREE LINKS OF THE CHAIN: ACHIEVING COLLABORATION AND INTERDEPENDENCE

Three aspects of the team need to be in place, like links of a chain, for a team to work collaboratively and interdependently. These aspects include the following three levels of the teaming work: the personal level, the discussion level, and the abstract/framing level. See Figure 9.1.

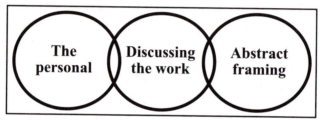

Figure 9.1. Three links of the chain: Achieving and maintaining collaboration and interdependence

The personal level represents the beliefs that each interpreter holds about his or her own work, independently as well as part of the team. The personal level has to do with deep psychological and emotional aspects of oneself, which may present underlying issues for relating to another interpreter during teaming (if these issues are not resolved). Interpreters may not discuss this level with each other because it is so deep and private (and includes such things as our self-talk), or interpreters may not be aware of these issues (as they may exist in the subconscious). And yet, these personal aspects of one's work can have a major impact on one's effectiveness as part of a team.

For example, an interpreter may have certain insecurities about attempting new tasks and strategies associated with teaming. This is a natural part of the process of change and should be expected as one figures out how to best work within the new "system" of teaming. Interpreters may also have mixed feelings about working closely with a particular interpreter due to past experiences in which they felt judged, and in which the so-called feedback they received was essentially a list of errors. Interpreters cannot be expected to quickly switch gears and trust the new process if they do not have the necessary techniques to move forward or do not have the experience that ensures to them the new approach works. Interpreters cannot overlook the impact of the personal level. A goal of any professional is to separate the personal from the professional, and yet doing so can be a real issue if someone has personal scars from past experiences with "teaming."

Recognizing any past pain or mixed feelings about teaming, and working through it, is part of the process of change. Damaged interpreters do not make for effective team interpreters. For instance, if someone is reluctant to make, or accept, corrections or switch roles as needed due to his or her own feelings of not wanting to look incompetent, that affects the team's ability to do its work. Interpreters need to work through the personal before they can put the team first. Just as interpreters with good mental health, clear boundaries, and positive self-esteem make for good interpreters, interpreters with these characteristics also can make for good team interpreters.

The next level, which is the discussion level, has to do with the ability of the team to discuss the team interpreting work.[3] The discussion (or processing) of the interpreting work is most effective when the interpreting work can be separated from the interpreters themselves, and when the interpreters relate well with each other and communicate openly with each other. As revealed by the two studies, the communication between the team members and their relationship are at the heart of their work together as a team. Teams are successful when they know how to talk to each other about their interpreting work. Such discussions are energizing because they enhance the team. This kind of discussion of the work is possible without the interpreters making each other feel badly about their work and, at the same time, without the interpreters being overly protective of each other's feelings. The focus is on growth, understanding, and change. This can be invigorating and can make for a closer bond between interpreters.

Interpreters love to discuss the interpreting process. When the focus is on discussing (rather than critiquing) the interpreting process in non-evaluative terms, the team assumes that each team member (and the team itself) is doing his or her best work and it is a matter of enhancing what they do together. The focus on *processing* rather than *critique* is key.

If the other member of the team seems reluctant to engage in a discussion, this reluctance may be lessened if the discussion is not seen as a critique (or traditional "feedback"). One technique that can be used to frame the discussion as *processing* is for an interpreter to start talking about his or her own interpreting process or decision-making process. The topic, then, becomes the subject at hand, rather than a "critique" in any sense of the word. This could pull the other interpreter into the discussion. Another technique is for an interpreter to engage with the other interpreter and to use active listening, and to support the other interpreter's exploration of their processing by participating in honest give and take.

Compare, for example, scenario #1 and scenario #2, both of which deal with the topic of affect (tone, emotion, or mood) in the interpretation. The scenarios illustrate the difference between providing traditional feedback and processing the work.

Scenario #1

Interpreter #1:   You didn't catch [*the Deaf person's*] affect. I think he was angry. You've got to really work on that.

Interpreter #2:   (grimacing): Okay. Thanks. That's good feedback for me.

Interpreter #1   (trying to make interpreter #2 feel better): What I usually try to do is to actually label in my own mind what the affect is: angry, excited, whatever, and then I'm more likely to convey it most of the time.

Interpreter #2:   Okay. I'll try that, or you could try to feed me.

Interpreter #1:   Yeah, I could. It seemed you were getting the information across okay, but I can feed you if you don't seem to be getting it.

Scenario #2

Interpreter A: I know [*the Deaf person*] was pretty upset today, but I don't think I conveyed that adequately in my interpretation.

Interpreter B: (looking at Interpreter A with interest) Okay. Talk to me about that.

Interpreter A: Well, I used phrases like "I'm not too happy about this," but I don't think it expressed his level of exasperation.

Interpreter B: That phrase seems to convey frustration, that's for sure; but it depends how we say it, I guess.

Interpreter A: That's it, exactly. I didn't *sound* upset.

Interpreter B: It makes you think about how vocal inflection and word choice combine to create the affect, doesn't it?

Interpreter A: Yeah. I think I was focusing on the words and not what my voice was doing. But I also don't want to overdo the vocal inflection either because that could alter the intent even more, but in the other direction. He wasn't "blow up" angry.

Interpreter B: I know what you mean. Do you remember how you interpreted the part where he said he was tired of having to revisit this issue? It seemed that he was upset at that point.

Interpreter A: That's a good question. Let me think… [*Discussion continues…*]

How the topic of affect is discussed in each scenario differs greatly. In the first scenario, the focus is on trying to improve or correct another interpreter's work. That interpreter may not be happy to hear the feedback, but tries to cooperate and "accept" the feedback. The interpreter who is giving the feedback (interpreter #1) proceeds to offer advice and, of course, the other interpreter feels the need to try to accept the suggestion as something to try. There is not really any give and take; this is basically a one-way conversation: one interpreter is supplying an evaluation/critique and informing the other interpreter about what to do, and the other person is supposed to be "open" to receiving this.

There are two main issues here. First, the relationship between them is being played out as a hierarchical relationship, much like an expert who points out strengths and weaknesses and offers pointers, and a learner who is supposed to be an open vessel that accepts the feedback and guidance without question. Perhaps this is the model that the interpreters have seen in their educational programs or in their professional development training as interpreters, but it really creates an odd and, I would argue, unhealthy dynamic between the two interpreters. Second, the feedback itself is focused on one interpreter's perspective of the other interpreter's performance or product. In this way, the observations may not be what would most benefit the recipient of the feedback. The feedback is an evaluation of strengths and weaknesses, and doesn't go much beyond that. This type of feedback is overly focused on evaluation of the interpreter's product and can ignore an individual's decision-making as an interpreter.

Sometimes such feedback can seem supportive because it is sugarcoated with empty phrases such as "You did a nice job." But at heart, this is still counterproductive to what the interpreters should be attending to as a team.

The discussion of affect in the second scenario is much different from the first. Interpreter A in the second scenario begins by talking about what he or she noticed and was thinking about. This provides an opening for the other interpreter to engage in discussion, and they both talk about their experience and thought process. What they are doing is identifying a topic (in this case, affect) and exploring the topic together. One of the elements that keeps the discussion on track is the use of specific examples. Interpreter A starts the discussion with a specific example and later interpreter B asks interpreter A for an example from another point in the interpretation. The examples, which are often part of the product (but could also be a decision an interpreter made or a question an interpreter has about how to manage or decide something), then become a case in point that can be used to discuss the process, and this approach enables the team to explore how they can best achieve equivalence in this area. Such discussions can also review the team's work together.

Three main differences exist between the second scenario and the first scenario.[4] First, their relationship is egalitarian rather than hierarchical. They are talking to each other as colleagues. One person is not necessarily an expert enlightening the other. They come to the discussion with the assumptions that they are both competent interpreters who know how to do this work, that they want to work together, and that they want to "think out loud" together in order to explore patterns or issues that arise. In contrast to the one-upmanship and judgment that is evident in scenario #1, the relationship in scenario #2 is between respected colleagues who are not using evaluative language and who are engaging in processing (or discussing) topics related to the interpreting process, the TL rendition, and the team interpreting process.

Second, the focus of the second scenario is more on the *process* than the *product*, and this is accomplished by discussing examples of the product, or examples of decisions an interpreter or the team has made. The focus, however, is on how interpreters make the decisions they do and how they manage the process (interpreting process and/or teaming process). This focus differs greatly from the focus on a prescribed list of features related to the interpreter's performance or the resulting product

(TL interpretation), which is the focus in the first scenario. The discussion in the second scenario is more fluid because the topics emerge from the common experience and can help lead the team to a better understanding of their own processing and decisions.

Third, the nature of the feedback or discussion is different in the two scenarios. The first scenario makes use of traditional feedback, but the second scenario makes use of a discussion, or processing, of the interpreting work. Not only is processing driven by discussing both the process and the product, it also requires that both interpreters be involved in the discussion. Both interpreters share their perspectives and both interpreters explore their own strategies and insight. In this way, the focus is on *understanding* rather than correcting. The end result is that processing increases the interpreters' ability to think more deeply and to apply this insight to the next interpreting assignment (or even to process it further at a later time with this interpreter or with someone else). The result is shared critical thinking that results in insight that is more immediately useful and more meaningful than the feedback session presented in scenario #1. When critique is set aside, neither interpreter feels that he or she is being supervised or evaluated. This distances the discussion from one's individual feelings and increases trust and respect between the interpreters.

Thus far, we have discussed two levels of team interpreting that need to be in place for an effective team within a collaborative and independent approach to teaming. We discussed the personal level and what interpreters may need to work through as they explore how they can successfully participate in a collaborative and interdependent team. One goal is to be self-aware of one's own baggage from one's previous experiences with team interpreting or one's previous view of teaming. This includes attending to one's own personal issues that may distract from a good, working (and cognitively intimate) relationship with another interpreter, so that one can focus on the needs of the team versus one's own individual emotional or psychological needs. We also discussed the ability of the team to discuss the team interpreting work, and we drew a contrast between providing *traditional feedback* and *processing* the work. *How* we talk about the work is important. Instead of inadvertently making others feel badly by feeding into a one-upmanship relationship, the goal is to *talk about*, and not evaluate, interpreting and teaming. This approach to processing not only increases the interpreters' understanding of their work, but it also builds trust and enriches the relationship between the interpreters. If there is a sense of one-upmanship, it can create a feeling of competition, which can counter the goal of working jointly as a team.[5]

The third level is the abstract way in which we frame our discussions. The personal level and the discussion level of teaming help us relate better with a team member, with whom we work closely. This third level has to do with the terminology we use and what models we use to discuss the work. A move from an "independent, but–" mentality to a "we" mentality requires a shift away from a focus on individual interpreters and assessment of their work; it requires a different stance toward teaming. Having a common way to talk about the interpreting work–in a more theoretical way–helps us accomplish that. For example, we have already discussed Colonomos's cognitive process model of interpreting (comprehending, representing, planning) and the Demand-Control Schema, which frames the interpreting task in terms of demands and controls (regarding paralinguistic, environmental, interpersonal, and intrapersonal aspects of our work).[6] Such models allow us to use a common vocabulary and to process topics at a deeper level. They also help us focus on the process and our decision-making, which is at the heart of processing our work as teams.

Interpreters in the field may also use other models to help them step back from the work and frame their processing of the work. Cokely and Colonomos both have models of the interpreting process that provide a detailed delineation of the cognitive process steps involved in interpreting, as well as key features of meaning, context, and discourse.[7] These can help interpreters process these aspects of their work. Cokely is also known for an approach to analyzing interpreting miscues (omissions, additions, substitutions, intrusions, and anomalies) that can assist interpreters in determining message equivalence.[8] Gish has an approach used for analyzing levels of meaning and discourse (goal, objective, unit, detail), and Colonomos has an approach to analyze the depth of processing that an interpreter is using to produce an interpretation (e.g., lexical, phrasal, sentential, and textual).[9] Winston and Monikowski have a discourse mapping approach that focuses on the coherence of texts in interpretation. Discourse mapping concentrates on content (topics, subtopics, themes, relationships, and events in the text), context (register, setting, audience, and speakers' goals), and form (e.g., discourse structures, transitions, and vocabulary).[10] In addition, Angelelli, Metzger, Roy, and Wadenjö provide ways to analyze the interaction among participants and the interpreter's role in the interaction, which includes both relaying information and coordinating the interaction.[11]

The field also has professional jargon that can be used to enhance the processing of a team's work. For example, teams can discuss register, affect, discourse, cultural adjustment, and dynamic equivalence; and teams can discuss how they are managing the interpreting process and how they determine dynamic equivalence given the specifics of a situation.[12] When teams focus on the interpretation in terms of decision-making, the discussion is not about any particular individual as an interpreter; it is one step removed. The discussion is about understanding the interpreting process, how interpreters manage the interpreting task, and how they make the decisions they do both in terms of the process and the product.

In addition to using a model or professional terminology, interpreters can use metaphors or analogies. A metaphor or an analogy can also be enlightening, and help the team step back and further explore its work. For example, an interpreter can say, "Interpreting is like making coffee. We have all of the ingredients from the source language to make the coffee, and we need to determine how to make the coffee. We also decide how to serve it. Do we serve it with cream and sugar, or do we serve it black? Well, it depends who we're making the coffee for. It depends on the target language users' expectations. If sugar is the politeness features of a language, I think I forgot the sugar in this interpretation!" Sometimes these indirect ways of discussing interpreting or teaming provide new insights into the team's work.

This book highlights many aspects of the team's work that teams can discuss. These aspects include the collaborative and interdependent view of teaming, what is covered in the pre-session, what makes for an effective team, the variety of teaming strategies, what modality and language to use, how teams can vary the way they work together, and how teams can achieve and maintain collaboration and interdependence.

Collaboration and interdependence do not just happen. They require all three links of the chain. They are the result of individuals who make personal change, who strive to improve their ability to discuss the team interpreting work, and make efforts to more abstractly frame and understand the work.

THOUGHT QUESTIONS 9.2
Three levels of collaboration and interdependence

1) Think about your own personal self-talk and what this means for you in terms of being able to work closely with another interpreter in a teaming situation. What are some personal characteristics that you may want to be aware of, so that they do not interfere with your teaming work or your ability to process the work? What are some personal characteristics that can benefit you and the team, and your processing of the team's work?

2) On a scale from 1 to 10, where would you place your tendency to use *traditional feedback* and where would you place your tendency to *process* the work? Discuss the implications of this graphic representation of your approach to discussing the work.

3) Name two or three ways in which you can increase your ability to process with another interpreter.

4) Identify two or three models or terms that you tend to use to help frame your discussions about interpreting and team interpreting. Are there other models or terms that you would like to explore to enhance your ability to process with others? Explain.

CONCLUSION

Team interpreting is like mountain climbing and yet it is not. For example, an interpreting team's tools do not consist of climbing equipment (of course). Our tools are not physical tools; they are what we bring to the interpreted event: our personal approach, our preparation for the assignment, our understanding of interpreting and teaming, our commitment, and our ability to analyze and review our work. As a team, we can strive to combine the tools of both interpreters into one cohesive whole that is stronger than its parts.

The two studies presented in this book have highlighted how a collaborative and interdependent approach to teaming can work, and what the barriers are that may prevent a team from working effectively together under this view. A new paradigm is exciting, yet it takes time and commitment to work within a new paradigm, and to develop the necessary techniques and to make progress in this type of joint work. The personal level, the discussion of the team interpreting work, and the abstract framing of the work are important features.

THOUGHT QUESTIONS 9.3
Further exploring collaboration and interdependence
CHAPTER REVIEW AND APPLICATION

1) This chapter has focused on how teams can achieve and maintain collaboration and interdependence as a team. What specifically can you do to increase your ability to *achieve* collaboration and interdependence within a team at each of the three levels: the personal level, the discussion level, and the abstract/framing level? And how specifically can interpreters with whom you team help *achieve* collaboration and interdependence with you?

2) Achieving collaboration and interdependence is the first step, but it is not an end in itself. What specifically can you do to increase your ability to *maintain* collaboration and interdependence within a team at each of the three levels: the personal level, the discussion level, and the abstract/framing level? And how specifically can interpreters with whom you team help *maintain* collaboration and interdependence with you?

ENDNOTES

[1] See Walker, 2007, for a discussion of team interpreting with the "we" mentality of "co-interpreting," as opposed to the "I" mentality of "co-working."

[2] See Kinsella, 1997, who mentions this notion of "Yes! and–," as opposed to "Yes, but–," when he discusses a conversation he had with interpreter Sharon Caserta regarding the enhancing nature of "feeds."

[3] See Colonomos, 2001; Shaw, 1989, for further discussion of processing one's interpreting work.

[4] Again, see Colonomos 2001; Shaw, 1989. Also, for examples of mentor-protégé discussions about a protégé's interpreting work, see Gordon & Magler, 2007; and for examples of teacher-student discussions about a student's interpreting work, see Gish, 1993.

[5] Richards, 2008.

[6] Colonomos, 1996; Dean & Pollard, 2001, and Pollard & Dean, 2008; respectively.

[7] Cokely, 1992; Colonomos, 1992.

[8] Cokely, 1992.

[9] Gish, 1987; Colonomos, 1995; respectively.

[10] Winston & Monikowski, 2000.

[11] Angelelli, 2003; Metzger, 1999; Roy, 2000a, 2000b; Wadensjö, 1998.

[12] See Halliday, 1978; Joos, 1968; for a discussion of register.

CHAPTER 10

A TEAM INTERPRETING MODEL:
COLLABORATION AND INTERDEPENDENCE AT WORK

A successful team beats with one heart.
—Unknown

Our focus throughout this book has been on the interaction and relationship between the interpreters in a team, and the two studies have informed much of our exploration of team interpreting. We have reviewed the research design of the two studies (Chapter 2); and we have looked at the theoretical aspects of team interpreting by clarifying the view of team interpreting as collaboration and interdependence (Chapter 1), and by describing the key components that make for an effective team (Chapter 3). We have looked at the pragmatic aspects of teaming by reviewing the topics and plans discussed during the pre-session (Chapter 4), and the strategies for feeding information as well as other teaming strategies (Chapters 5 and 6). We explored team interpreting further by looking at the decision regarding what modality and language to use during teaming (Chapter 7), how different teams function differently (Chapter 8), and how teams can achieve and maintain collaboration and interdependence (Chapter 9). In this final chapter, we will pull all of these topics together and propose a model of team interpreting, to complete our exploration of the process interpreters undergo when they team together using a collaborative and interdependent approach.

We have stressed that team interpreting is not just about what is produced as the product (the target language), even though a dynamically equivalent TL rendition is the goal of the team. Rather, team interpreting is centered on the *process* of working together, and this process can occur at three main times: during the pre-session, during the interpretation, and during the post-session.[1]

The source language (SL) is not part of the teaming process, *per se.* More accurately, it receives the attention of the team and is what the team is working to convey in the alternate language when interpreting. The TL is the end product that results from the team's interpreting work. It is also not part of the process; it is the *result* of the process. Both the SL and the TL appear as a linguistic expression of meaning, or *form*; what occurs within the interpreters' brains and what interaction there is between them is the *process*. So, the model covers the pre-session (collaborating beforehand), the interpretation (collaborating and interpreting interdependently during the interpretation), and the post-session (processing the teaming work afterwards). See Figure 10.1. We will review each of these three types of interactions in turn. When we consider the interpretation, we will discuss the SL and the TL as well.

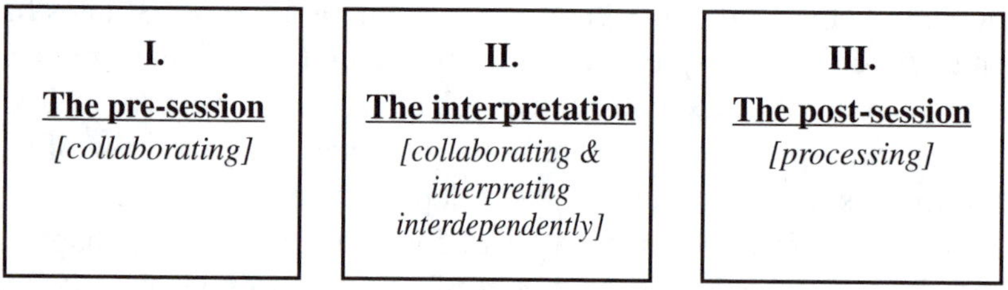

I. **The pre-session** *[collaborating]*	II. **The interpretation** *[collaborating & interpreting interdependently]*	III. **The post-session** *[processing]*

Figure 10.1. The three types of interactions that teams have when working together

THOUGHT QUESTIONS 10.1
Form vs. process

1) The three types of interactions in the model deal with *process*. Define *process* in your own words.

2) The SL and the TL of the model deal with *form*. Define *form* in your own words.

3) Name three key components of the teaming *process* that you want to keep foremost in your mind.

4) Name three key components of *form* (in the SL and/or the TL) that you want to keep foremost in your mind.

THE PRE-SESSION (COLLABORATING BEFOREHAND)

The pre-session provides the team with an opportunity to discuss the team's upcoming work. During the pre-session, the team builds rapport and connects in a way that establishes or maintains their relationship, and the team then begins collaborating on the interpreting assignment. They gather and share information, and assist each other in building a schema, i.e., creating a working informational framework that includes necessary knowledge, the kinds of discourse to expect, and general goals of the participants. They discuss what they predict or anticipate will happen either in terms of meaning, in terms of the dynamics of the situation, or in terms of their own work together; and they share particular needs they have. The team benefits most when it is focused on specific meaning-based issues to ensure dynamic equivalence (ensuring a contextually-rich interpretation), and on teaming issues that can help them team together during the interpreting assignment. Teams can interpret most effectively when they discuss, and make decisions about, specific ways that they can work together, including strategies they can use, when and how they will function in the monitor and lead interpreter roles (including the use of information feeds and other teaming strategies), and the best placement of the team or dealing with other logistical issues.

Teams may also interact with others in the situation during this time in order to help them better prepare by asking for additional information. For example, they may ask for an agenda, handout, or PowerPoint; they may talk to a speaker about the forthcoming presentation or meeting; they may negotiate logistics with participants (lighting needs, etc.); or they may ask if any particular media (such as a video presentation) will be used. The pre-session sets the stage for the teaming work, and it is in the pre-session where team interpreting really begins. See Figure 10.2.

The pre-session [collaborating]

Discussing the team's upcoming work
- Building rapport/Connecting
- Gathering/Sharing information
- Building a schema
- Predicting/Anticipating
- Sharing needs
- Discussing strategies & making decisions
- Discussing monitor & lead roles (information feeds & other teaming strategies)
- Managing logistics
- Determining placement

Figure 10.2. Key features of the pre-session [collaborating]

THOUGHT QUESTIONS 10.2
Collaborating beforehand: The pre-session

1) Identify two features that you tend to think about as you prepare for an interpreting assignment when you work alone (e.g., the speaker's goal, cultural mediation, managing interaction). Discuss the benefits of discussing these features with a team interpreter before teaming.

2) Which of the information feeds (*confirmations, TL feeds [corrections, enhancements]*, and *message feeds*) or other teaming strategies (*switching roles* and *collaborating*) do you think are important for the team to discuss beforehand? Explain. Also, which of these do you think do need not to be discussed beforehand? Explain.

3) What is the best way to discuss modality and language usage in the pre-session? Explain.

4) Explain how interpreters decide where to position themselves, and explain with whom the interpreter may consult about this decision.

THE INTERPRETATION
(DURING THE INTERPRETING WORK TOGETHER)

When the team is working together during the interpreting assignment, the focus is mostly on working interdependently on the interpreting task. The collaboration that occurs during the pre-sessions–as well as the past experiences the team members have with teaming and interpreting, and with working with each other–affect their joint interpreting process. Teaming during the interpretation involves collaborating and working interdependently to convey in the TL what was conveyed in the SL. See Figure 10.3.

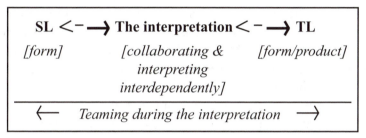

Figure 10.3. Teaming during the interpretation

THE SOURCE LANGUAGE (FORM)

Simply said, the *source language* is what primary participants say. What is not as simple to describe is what is *meant* by what is said. The SL has many components, and these components need to be understood by an interpreting team before it can express the true meaning of the SL in the TL. The most evident component of the SL is the content, or information, expressed. However, a speaker conveys much more than facts. The speaker, for example, has a particular goal in mind, which is what the speaker is trying to accomplish by the utterance, and can include such functions as the following: to persuade, to educate, to entertain, to elicit a response, and so on. Additionally, speakers communicate how they perceive themselves in the situation and how they see their relationship with others; in short, they convey social meaning.[2] Register, which is the degree of psychological distance or relative casualness/formality, and linguistic politeness, which involves decisions regarding how to express utterances due to the desire to save face and maintain relationships, are two linguistic features that are characteristic of the social level of language.[3]

Affect and cultural overlays are two other features of the SL. Affect is the mood, tone, or emotion that is being conveyed, and cultural overlays include the behaviors, thoughts, or assumptions one has from one's own cultural upbringing. The two differ in that affect has to do with the expression of a specific tone or feeling within a specific situation; whereas, cultural overlays are more general and relate to the worldview one has developed from having grown up with certain norms, traditions, values, and beliefs.[4]

Another level of language meaning is the textual level. The textual level has to do with language usage above the sentence level, and includes how current utterances relate to previous utterances or to forthcoming utterances. One level of textual analysis is the structural components of discourse, e.g., how a lecture, narrative, discussion, or interview is structured. Another level of textual analysis has to do with the interactive nature of discourse, and focuses more on how participants take turns in interaction, i.e., how they signal the end of a turn and signal wanting a turn. Interpreters may find it necessary to manage the interaction, especially when participants' talk overlaps, in which case, interpreters may need to indicate to participants that they can go ahead and speak, or that they should wait to speak.[5]

Additionally, participants communicate who is saying what, i.e., who the speaker is and who the addressee is. This orientation of the utterance is called *footing* and is evident when someone is speaking for him/herself, is reporting what someone else has said, or is addressing only certain addressees and not others. Interpreters, for example, change footing when they speak for themselves and ask for clarification or ask someone to repeat an utterance, rather than convey the interaction between primary participants. Generally, the interpreter conveys the footing of "one speaker talking to another (or a group of people)," but sometimes the interpreter conveys the footing of "the interpreter talking to a speaker (or speakers)." Such utterances are not renditions; they are additional contributions to the interaction initiated by the interpreter.[6]

In sum, there are at least four levels of meaning conveyed in an utterance.[7] These are the following:

> Content
> Speaker's goal (function)
> Social meaning
> Textual meaning

These four levels of meaning comprise the overall sense conveyed in a SL message, and each can be broken down further. The SL includes not only utterances; it also includes, and is influenced by, participants' specific behaviors, interpreter-initiated utterances, and the dynamics of the situation. An interpreting team's goal is to convey all four levels of meaning of the SL into the TL. See Figure 10.4.

> ## *The SL [form]*
>
> ### *What is said*
> - Content
> - Speaker's goal
> - Social meaning
> - Textual meaning
> - Interaction & footing
> - Affect
> - Cultural overlays
> - Interpreter-initiated utterances
> - Behaviors/Dynamics

Figure 10.4. Key features of the source language [form]

THOUGHT QUESTIONS 10.3
What is meant: The source language

1) Come up with an example of an interesting, or challenging, utterance that was said during an interpreting assignment and, for that utterance, identify the following: the *content, speaker's goal, social meaning,* and *textual meaning*. Discuss which level, or levels, of meaning were more prominent in determining the speaker's intent.

2) As an interpreter, are there certain features that are presented in Figure 10.4 that you need to focus on the most? Explain.

3) Which of these features lend themselves to more collaborating during the pre-session and which of them lend themselves more to collaborating/working interdependently during the interpretation? Explain.

THE TEAMING PROCESS DURING THE INTERPRETATION

Teaming during the interpretation involves a negotiation of the team's ongoing work with each other and the participants, and results in the TL rendition. Teams strive to maintain rapport and their connection, but primarily focus on collaborating and working interdependently in order to complete the shared goal.

Although the monitoring view of teaming has been overly focused on the relaying of information, interpreters focus not only on the accuracy of the information in the TL (i.e., complete and correct content), they focus equally on dynamic equivalence. Dynamic equivalence, or message equivalence, involves the speaker's goal, social meaning, and textual meaning. The team is working together to attend to the context and cultural overlays to determine a speaker's intent beyond facts and details, and addresses questions such as the following: What are the thoughts the speaker is trying to convey? What is the speaker trying to accomplish in terms of his/her impact, or in terms of the discourse or interaction? What is the speaker saying about his/her relationship with the addressee(s) and what are the social messages the speaker is trying to get across? Is the speaker being friendly, off-putting, overly polite, disrespectful, or forceful? How is a speaker organizing the presentation? Is the speaker leaving something implicit that needs to be explicit in the TL, or stating something explicitly that is best left implicit in the TL? Is a speaker finished talking, wanting to talk, indicating agreement, or using listening behaviors (backchanneling) to encourage someone else to continue talking? Such questions are part of dynamic equivalence, which involves meaning beyond literal content. Teams of interpreters, as with individual interpreters, attend to such levels of meaning for a rich, dynamically equivalent interpretation.

We have mentioned that interpreters interact with participants before an interpretation begins by asking for additional information, by asking about particular media needs, or by asking about any specific logistical or situational needs. During an interpretation, interpreters may also interact with participants for these same reasons or for other reasons as well. For example, interpreters may ask someone to wait so that they can catch up in the interpretation or to clarify a point in the TL, may ask someone to clarify something that was said, may ask a participant to go ahead with a turn or to hold a turn, or may inform a TL addressee about something in the environment that may be important for that person to know about (such as another participant's manner or tone, or another participant's being preoccupied by something else in the situation).[8] An interpreter interacts with the SL participant(s) in these ways, which indicates that the SL is not a frozen, given entity. The SL is part of the dynamics and an interpreter, or an interpreting team, may affect the SL for the benefit of the interpreting process by affecting either the clarity of the message or the interaction of participants. In this way, interpreters and interpreting teams make decisions (both individually and together) that can affect both meaning and the dynamics of the situation.

The team needs to determine (either in the pre-session or on the spot) whether the lead interpreter or the monitor interpreter will interact with the SL participant(s) in these instances. Neither study looked at this question; however, it is typical in practice for the interpreter in the lead role to turn to the interpreter in the monitor role to see if the monitor can provide the needed information or if the monitor can switch roles, as needed. If not, then the lead interpreter may switch footing and produce an interpreter-initiated utterance, by speaking for him/herself rather than rendering the speaker's meaning. Interpreter-initiated utterances can be used to manage the interaction (asking someone to wait, to take a turn, or to hold a turn, for example), or to manage the message (by asking someone to clarify, to go back to a previous point, or to pause or slow down). As with interpreters working alone, teams also manage the interaction and render the message in an interpretation. The lighter arrows in Figure 10.3 refer back to the SL and indicate that the team interpreting process does not just move forward through the steps. The team also may move backward to a previous step (or steps) at times. The team interpreting process (and interpreting process) is dynamic in this way.

In addition, team members may make accommodations in two other ways. They may alter how they work together to better meet the needs of the team, as when changing the timing of one's information feeds or other teaming strategies, as occurred with one of the teams in the videotape study. They may also make changes to the environment, as was reported in the survey, in that interpreters may adjust the lighting or the seating arrangement, may bring each other water, or may make other changes to the surroundings. Figure 10.5 illustrates the various aspects of the team interpreting process during the interpretation.

The team interpreting process [collaborating and interpreting interdependently]

Negotiating the team's work
- Maintaining rapport/connection
- Working interdependently and collaboratively on the interpreting (CRP) process to achieve dynamic equivalence & information accuracy
- Making decisions (individually or together)
- Negotiating & performing monitor & lead roles (information feeds & other teaming strategies)
- Using interpreter-initiated utterances (interacting with speakers)
- Making accommodations

Figure 10.5. Key features of the team interpreting process [collaborating and interpreting interdependently]

THE TARGET LANGUAGE (FORM/PRODUCT)

The *target language* is the resulting product of the team's efforts. As we discussed with the SL, there are two types of equivalence with which interpreters concern themselves: information accuracy and dynamic equivalence. Information accuracy has to do with quantity, i.e., the degree to which the amount of information (content) intended in the SL is conveyed in the TL. Dynamic equivalence has to do with quality, i.e., the degree to which the deep level of meaning (speaker's goal, social meaning, and textual meaning) is conveyed in the TL. Of course, both quality and quantity are important in an interpretation, and each of these may become more salient in some situations than in others. Compare, for example, a person who is relating an emotionally upsetting experience and a person who is explaining the detailed steps to an algebraic equation. Quality (overall meaning and intent) in the first example is foregrounded, and quantity (getting as many of the details as possible) in the second example is foregrounded. This is but one way in which an interpreter, or an interpreting team, needs to consider how to convey the speaker's goals in the situation.

Cultural meaning is another consideration, and cultural adjustments need to be made in the TL as needed. Such adjustments tend to be made more when the focus is on quality (overall sense) as opposed to quantity (more factual-based information); although both likely require some cultural adjustment. In addition, speakers always leave some information implicit, but what is left implicit varies depending on what language is used and the situation one is in, and an interpreter needs to determine whether to make some content more explicit or more implicit in the TL. Affect, too, is an important consideration in interpretation; the tenor of a text or the emotional stance taken by a speaker is an important feature of dynamic equivalence. How someone says something is sometimes more important than what they say, e.g., consider again the two scenarios above: the person who is emotionally upset vs. the person who is explaining an algebraic equation. Although these two examples highlight the difference between dynamic equivalence and information accuracy, neither dynamic equivalence nor information accuracy strictly characterizes any situation. Interpreters, and interpreting teams, need to determine to what degree each is to be given emphasis in the TL rendition.

The primary goal of the team of interpreters is to convey the four levels of meaning (content, speaker's goal, social meaning, and textual meaning). At the textual level, the connectedness of the discourse is the focus, whether the TL is a narrative, lecture, dialogue, or another kind of interaction. Appropriate turn-taking regulators and overall textual meaning (such as transitional markers or discourse markers) need to be conveyed by the team in order to preserve the intent of the SL speakers.

Interpreters also interact directly with participants at times, and such interpreter-initiated utterances involve a change in footing. Such changes in footing indicate that the interpreting team (or interpreter) is part of the interaction. However, the team plays a particular, limited role in the interaction: as relayer of meaning and manager of the interaction for purposes of conveying people's intent. When a member of the interpreting team changes footing by producing an interpreter-initiated utterance, this utterance is part of the form/product of the interpretation. It is one way in which interpreters may alter the form of the TL. In addition, participants' behaviors and the dynamics of the situation are all part of the TL. Figure 10.6 illustrates all of the key features of the TL form/product.

> ## *The TL [form/product]*
>
> ### *What the team produces*
> - Dynamic equivalence (speaker's goal,
>   social meaning, textual meaning)
> - Information accuracy (content)
> - Cultural adjustments
> - Affect
> - Interaction & footing
> - Interpreter-initiated utterances
> - Behaviors/Dynamics

Figure 10.6. Key features of the target language [form/product]

THE POST-SESSION (PROCESSING AFTERWARDS)

Committed teams of interpreters strive to process their teaming work afterwards. This can occur immediately afterwards, later over coffee, or even on the phone. All three teams in the videotape study mentioned that they tend to process afterwards and several of the interpreters in the survey also mentioned meeting with the other interpreter afterwards. The rapport and connection between team members is reinforced and maintained by such interactions, and this rapport and connection also allows the team to be open with each other and to process two main facets of the team interpreting work.

First, teams can review and process their work together. They can discuss the effectiveness of the pre-session, their modality and language usage, the strategies they used during the interpretation, and their teamwork overall, as well as features of the SL and the TL in terms of dynamic equivalence and information accuracy.

Second, teams can begin to look ahead and make progress forward in terms of their own insights into the work of the team. Each interpreter can identify what was learned about him/herself, and the team can discover things about each other and their teaming together. They can rethink strategies, enhance strategies, come up with new strategies, or commit to certain strategies, and discover insights into their working relationship in terms of collaborating and working interdependently with each other. See Figure 10.7.

The post-session [processing]

Processing the team's work (process & product)
- Maintaining rapport/connection
- Reviewing/Processing:
    1) the pre-session
    2) the teaming process
    3) strategies & decisions
    4) the SL & TL/product
- Thinking ahead/Progressing forward:
    1) what was learned about oneself, the other
       interpreter, & teaming
    2) strategies & insights for next time

Figure 10.7. Key features of the post-session [processing]

A MODEL: TEAM INTERPRETING AS THREE TYPES OF INTERACTION

Much of the literature has focused on the team interpreting process during the interpretation. In fact, most of the literature has focused on how teams can support each other by feeding information, and this view gives great focus to information accuracy. This view is limited in two major respects. First, the team interpreting that occurs during the actual interpretation is, of course, the most obvious teaming interaction, but it is but one type of interaction (of three) that is part of the team interpreting process. In fact, much of the team interpreting process happens before and after the actual interpreting work. Second, there is much more going on during the interpretation itself. Team interpreting is not just about monitoring and repairing the TL rendition.

The model of team interpreting, presented in Figure 10.8, illustrates the three main types of interactions that are involved in team interpreting. All three types of interactions may not always occur, as when the team cannot meet beforehand or afterwards. But for teams to collaborate and to benefit from their work together, all three interactions need to occur over time, even if the pre-session or the post-session is abbreviated or occurs on the telephone.

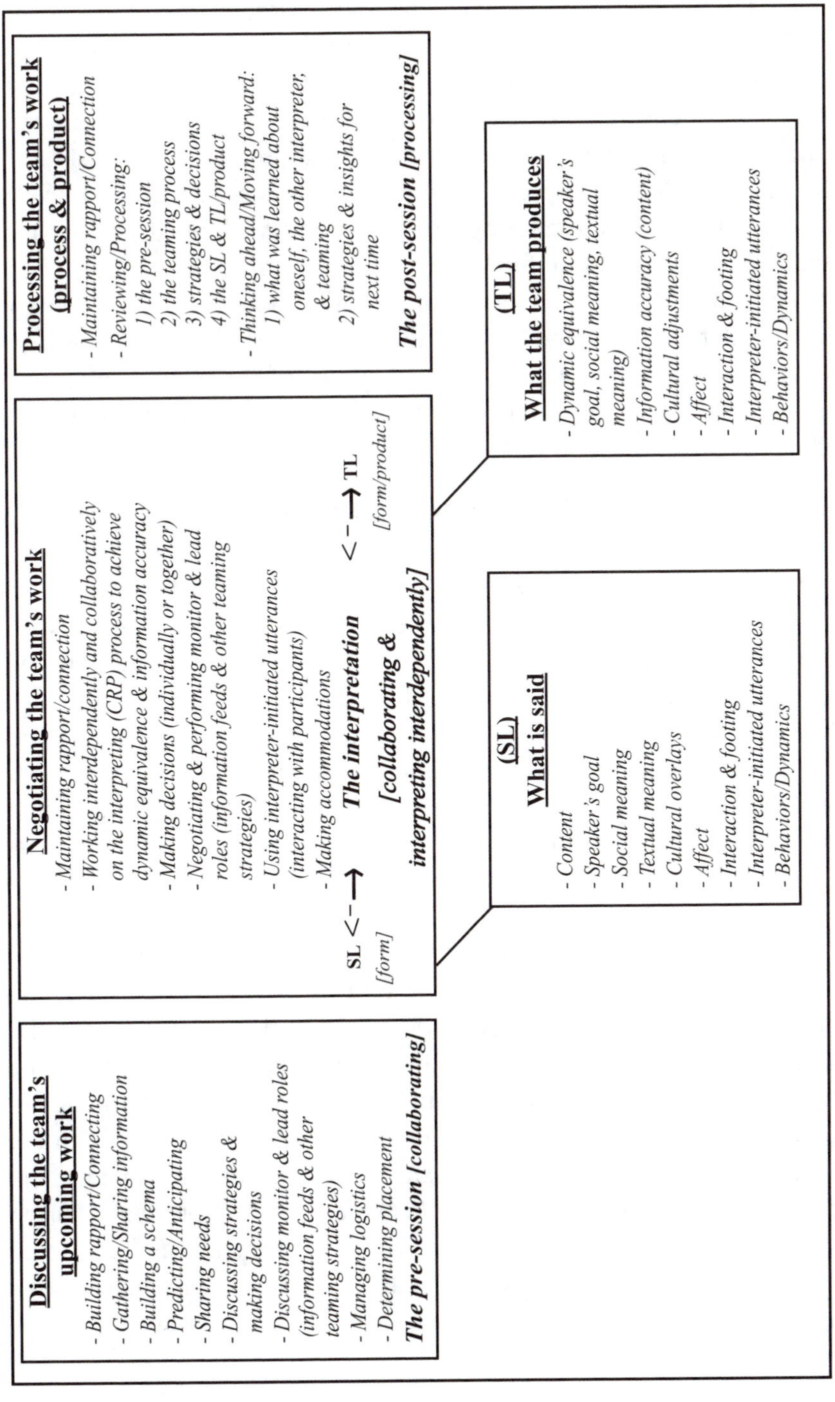

Discussing the team's upcoming work

- Building rapport/Connecting
- Gathering/Sharing information
- Building a schema
- Predicting/Anticipating
- Sharing needs
- Discussing strategies & making decisions
- Discussing monitor & lead roles (information feeds & other teaming strategies)
- Managing logistics
- Determining placement

The pre-session [collaborating]

Negotiating the team's work

- Maintaining rapport/connection
- Working independently and collaboratively on the interpreting (CRP) process to achieve dynamic equivalence & information accuracy
- Making decisions (individually or together)
- Negotiating & performing monitor & lead roles (information feeds & other teaming strategies)
- Using interpreter-initiated utterances (interacting with participants)
- Making accommodations

SL <--->   **The interpretation**   <---> TL
[form]   *[collaborating &*   *[form/product]*
       interpreting interdependently]

Processing the team's work (process & product)

- Maintaining rapport/Connection
- Reviewing/Processing:
  1) the pre-session
  2) the teaming process
  3) strategies & decisions
  4) the SL & TL/product
- Thinking ahead/Moving forward:
  1) what was learned about oneself, the other interpreter, & teaming
  2) strategies & insights for next time

The post-session [processing]

(SL)
What is said

- Content
- Speaker's goal
- Social meaning
- Textual meaning
- Cultural overlays
- Affect
- Interaction & footing
- Interpreter-initiated utterances
- Behaviors/Dynamics

(TL)
What the team produces

- Dynamic equivalence (speaker's goal, social meaning, textual meaning)
- Information accuracy (content)
- Cultural adjustments
- Affect
- Interaction & footing
- Interpreter-initiated utterances
- Behaviors/Dynamics

Figure 10.8. The team interpreting process: Collaboration and interdependence at work

Before interpreting process models emerged, interpreters focused on the SL and TL, and didn't have a good sense of how they could best accomplish the "invisible" work that takes place in their heads (cognitively) to achieve an equivalent, cohesive TL rendition. The interpreting process models have helped our field better understand how we process cognitively and reach decisions when interpreting. The goal of this book has been to do likewise for the team interpreting process. We have looked beyond the SL, the TL, and information feeds to how the team prepares and connects beforehand, how the team works collaboratively and interdependently during the interpretation, and how the team processes its work afterwards. These are all types of interactions that are part of the team interpreting process; team interpreting is far more inclusive and offers much more to a team than a narrow view would suggest.

IMPLICATIONS AND FUTURE RESEARCH

The findings of the two studies presented here clarify how teams of interpreters can effectively work together to achieve a successful interpretation, and provide a framework for studying team interpreting that can be replicated or adapted for future research. The results have implications for the field of interpretation, interpreter education, and language study more generally. In addition, team interpreting is a rich area of research, and research is needed to further explore at least three related areas: the field's view of how a team can work together, practical aspects of team interpreting, and other, more specific features of teaming.

The findings of the two studies have implications for three related areas. First, the results of these studies suggest that the field of interpretation is undergoing a paradigm shift to a view of team interpreting based on ongoing collaboration and interdependence. With this change comes the need to explore the implications in one's own teaming work. It is one thing to state that a new view of teaming has emerged; it is another to actually work out the specifics in terms of one's day-to-day work in the field. Just as the field continues to examine and further understand the cultural mediation and ally metaphors (models) of interpreting, and the interpreting process, team interpreting takes introspection and continual processing by teams. This is especially true due to the fact that no two teams are the same and no two interpreting assignments are the same.

Research is needed to further flesh out the collaborative and interdependent view of team interpreting.

Second, the model presented in this chapter, and the various topics presented in the book, provide a framework for interpreter education. Interpreter education programs can use this model in the education of advanced students. Based on the research here, it is clear that team interpreting should be introduced when students have basic competencies in interpretation because teaming requires these competencies as a foundation. Also, there are implications for students' field experience (practicum) work. Students would benefit most from observing experienced teams of interpreters and from working in teams with qualified, experienced interpreters. At the same time, these mentorship opportunities need to consider the disparity between the skills of the student and mentor, so that the needs of the primary participants in the interpreting situation can be met.

The team interpreting model presented here can also be used for continuing education for professional interpreters. In addition to helping frame how interpreters approach their work, ongoing training and coursework can use this framework to structure these educational opportunities.

Third, the majority of interpreters are second language users of ASL, so there are also implications for second language learning. Interpreting teams need to explore all four levels of language usage in their working languages, so ASL coursework in interpreting programs (and continuing education) should be sure to address content, speaker's goal, social meaning, and textual meaning.

There is also a need for research in three main areas. First, although the research presented here has clarified how teams can conceptualize team interpreting in terms of a collaborative and interdependent process, and what makes for an effective interpreting team (Chapters 1 and 3), research on specific areas of these two topics is warranted and would provide additional insight into what constitutes effective team interpreting. Specific areas include (1) interpreting assignments that currently do not tend to employ an interpreting team that may best be served by having a team of interpreters, (2) how the field continues to change its view of team interpreting, and (3) further clarification of specific components of the four features of effective teaming: personal characteristics/skills, relationship/communication, philosophy/schema, and commitment/trust.

Second, further research on specific practical aspects of team interpreting can be pursued. The topics and strategies discussed in the pre-session (Chapter 4) and the types of information feeds and other teaming strategies (Chapters 5 and 6) have been delineated here. However, research can enlighten what topics teams may not discuss enough in the pre-session; *how* and *when* teams can best utilize specific teaming strategies; the effectiveness of strategies and which need to be discussed beforehand to be more effective; how teams can more effectively monitor each other's interpreting (CRP) process, as well as other aspects of the team interpreting environment (including paralinguistic, environmental, interpersonal, and intrapersonal demands and controls); how teams can provide healthy emotional and psychological support of each other; and when information feeds or changing roles can be most effective. Also, two teaming strategies were used the least in the videotape study (TL feeds and switching roles); research can clarify if the field would benefit from using these strategies more often.

Third, there are many other potential areas of research. These include the following: the impact of gender or ethnic differences on teaming, how Deaf-hearing teams work together, how having English as the SL affects the team's work, how interpreting teams manage interpreted interaction, how the pre-session varies depending on the type of assignment, how ethical and professional decisions are made by a team, what interpreters can do when they have differing expectations and approaches to the teaming work, how teams can best work with consumers (during the interpretation, as well as in pre- and post-sessions), and how nonverbal communication is used by teams to signal each other when team interpreting.

In addition, many questions remain regarding other areas of team interpreting. The book explored how teams can determine which modality and language to use during team interpreting (Chapter 7), how teams may function differently (Chapter 8), how teams can achieve and maintain collaboration and interdependence (Chapter 9), and a model of team interpreting that provides an overview of the elements of team interpreting (this chapter). However, there are lingering questions about each of these areas. Possible areas of research include the variables that determine which modality and language is used by a team (written, spoken, signed, or nonverbal), the team's relationship with participants (especially Deaf people) and the impact of such relationships on the team's ability to do its work; how teams manage their interaction with participants (which of the team members asks for clarification, for example); when the Open Process Model should be utilized and when it is best not to use such a model; and how differing cultural views (independence vs. collectivism) are realized within the team and how these affect the team's relationship with participants. Research can also clarify other ways in which team members can adapt to the specific needs of the team and the context, or ways in which teams may overcompensate, e.g., may offer certain feeds or other teaming strategies too much. Research can also further elaborate specific aspects of what allows teams to achieve and maintain collaboration and interdependence at the levels of the personal, discussion of the work, and the abstract framing of the work; and can further investigate the many features of the team interpreting model presented here: specifics related to the pre-session, the interpretation (including the SL and TL), and the post-session. For example, the field would benefit from research on what teams do if there is little or no time for a pre-session and/or post-session.

Many of the questions that require further research can be clarified by either qualitative or quantitative research. At the same time, many of these questions will be answered in the everyday work of interpreters. The two studies here have shed light on the team interpreting process and have clarified many areas that have previously not been explored. At the same time, team interpreting continues to be a rich area of research.

CONCLUSION

Working in teams is a complex process, and one that benefits the interpreters and the effectiveness of the interpretation when it works well. The collaborative and interdependent view presented in this book, and the results of the two studies, have helped clarify what is needed for a team to successfully work together. As interpreters, we create the team, and we can truly create the types of teams we want. This book has attempted to clarify what teams of interpreters can be and how we can achieve effective team interpreting. The rest is up to each of us in our day-to-day work and in our processing of team interpreting with each other.

THOUGHT QUESTIONS 10.4
The team interpreting model
CHAPTER REVIEW AND APPLICATION

1) Identify two or three aspects of the team interpreting model presented in this chapter that you would like to explore further. Discuss how you plan to explore these particular aspects of teaming.

2) If you were to research an area of team interpreting, what would you choose to research? How would you go about researching this area?

3) Review the chapter titles of the book and, for each chapter, discuss your thoughts on these areas of team interpreting now that you have explored them in depth (see the list in *italics* below).

   Topics covered in this book:
   • *Team interpreting: Defining what we do (Chapter 1)*
   • *Investigating team interpreting (Chapter 2)*
   • *Effective interpreting teams (Chapter 3)*
   • *The pre-session (Chapter 4)*
   • *Strategies for feeding information (Chapter 5)*
   • *Other teaming strategies (Chapter 6)*
   • *Modality and language usage (Chapter 7)*
   • *Different teams, different working styles (Chapter 8)*
   • *Achieving and maintaining collaboration and interdependence (Chapter 9)*
   • *A team interpreting model: Collaboration and interdependence at work (Chapter 10)*

ENDNOTES

1   Several authors have discussed these types of interactions that occur during the pre-session and the post-session, although they often use different terms (as discussed in the Preface). These authors include Cerney, 2005; Cohen-Gilbert & D'Entremont, 2007; Jones, 2007; Walker, 1994; among others; as well as Cogen, Forestal, Hills, & Hollrah, 2006, who focus their work on Deaf-hearing teams.

2   See Hoza, 2007a, for a discussion of content, function/speaker meaning, social meaning, and textual meaning (textual meaning is discussed below).

3   See Joos, 1968; Halliday, 1978; for a review of register; and see Hoza, 2007a; Roush, 2007; for a discussion of linguistic politeness in ASL and English, and Hoza, 1999, 2007b, for a discussion of linguistic politeness in interpretation.

4   See Mindess, 2006, for further information regarding key cultural differences between Deaf people and hearing people.

5   Roy, 2000a.

6   Metzger, 1999; Wadensjö, 1998.

7   Hoza, 2007a.

8   Angelelli, 2003; Berk-Seligson, 1990; Metzger, 1999; Roy, 2000a, 2000b (whose focus is on how interpreters manage turn-taking and overlap); Wadensjö, 1998.

APPENDIX I

APPENDIX I. INTERVIEW QUESTIONS

Background information:
1) a. How old are you?
   b. What interpreting certification(s) do you hold? What year did you receive it/them?
   c. How many years of interpreting experience do you have? – and in what kinds of settings?
   d. How many years of team interpreting experience do you have? –and in what kinds of settings?
   e. How long have you worked with [*the other interpreter*] as a team interpreter? –and in what kinds of settings?

Questions regarding team interpreting in general – and with the other interpreter:
2) a. What are three things that are most important for team interpreting work to be successful?
   b. Do you generally prefer to team interpret with the same interpreters or not? Explain.
   c. What makes for a good team interpreter?

   \-

   d. Do you feel you team interpret well with [*the other interpreter*]? Explain.
   e. What are some ways you and [*the other interpreter*] could improve your team interpreting work, if any? Explain.

   \-

   f. What are three things that can lessen the effectiveness of team interpreting work?
   g. Are there any interpreters that you would rather not team interpret with? Explain.
   h. What makes for a poor team interpreter?

Questions regarding this team interpreting assignment:
3) a. How well do you think this team interpreting assignment went, and why? (Discuss; give examples.)
   b. What was most effective about this team interpreting assignment? Give some examples.

c. What would <u>you</u> do differently if you were to do this assignment again? –or if <u>you</u> were to team interpret with this interpreter again?

d. What would you like <u>this interpreter</u> to do differently if you were to do this assignment with this interpreter again? –or if you were to team interpret with <u>this interpreter</u> again? –what would (or could) you do to help make this change happen?

e. Can you give examples of things you may have learned about team interpreting from this team interpreting assignment (if not discussed already) that you can apply to your other team interpreting work? (Give examples.)

Questions regarding actual videotaped excerpts:

4) *NOTE: The questions for this part of the interview were more organic and emerged from the actual team interpreting assignment, and involved questions regarding excerpts from the videotaped interpreting work. Between six and eight excerpts were shown to the interpreter being interviewed, and the following were explored:*

a. What do you think (or see) was happening here?

b. Why do you think you–or the other interpreter–initiated this (interaction or strategy)? What was your–or the other interpreter's–goal at this time?

c. Why do you think the other interpreter–or you–responded as s/he did? What was his/her goal at this time?

d. Was this interaction effective? What made it effective or not? –What are some other possible options/strategies in this kind of situation? Discuss.

e. Is there anything else you would like to say about this excerpt? Explain.

Wrap-up questions:

5) a. Is there anything else that you would like to share about your experience with team interpreting experience in this particular team interpreting assignment? Explain.

b. Is there anything else that you would like to share about your experience with team interpreting experience in general? Explain.

APPENDIX II

APPENDIX II. SURVEY ON TEAM INTERPRETING

UNH SurveyCat
Survey on Team Interpreting

Thank you for your willingness to answer the questions on this survey.
You can expect the survey to take approximately 15 minutes to complete.

PERSONAL BACKGROUND QUESTIONS

Please provide the following information. Unless otherwise indicated, only one option is allowed for each question.

1) Your gender:
   - ○ Male
   - ○ Female

2) Your age (in years):

3) Your hearing status:
   - ○ Hearing
   - ○ Hearing coda (child of Deaf adults(s))
   - ○ Deaf
   - ○ Hard-of-hearing
   - ○ Other

4) Your race/ethnicity: (Select all that apply.)
   - ❑ European ancestry
   - ❑ African ancestry
   - ❑ Hispanic or Latino ancestry
   - ❑ Asian or Pacific Islander ancestry
   - ❑ American Indian or Alaskan Native ancestry
   - ❑ Other

5) State you live in:
   AL

6) Your highest level of education:
- ○ High school diploma/GED
- ○ Associate's degree
- ○ Bachelor's degree
- ○ Master's degree
- ○ Doctoral degree
- ○ Other [   ]

PROFESSIONAL BACKGROUND QUESTIONS

Please provide the following information. As before, unless otherwise indicated, only one option is allowed for each question.

7) How many years of professional interpreting experience do you have?
- ○ 1-5 years
- ○ 6-10 years
- ○ 11-15 years
- ○ 16-20 years
- ○ 21-25 years
- ○ 26 years or more

8) For how many years have you been nationally certified?
- ○ 1-5 years
- ○ 6-10 years
- ○ 11-15 years
- ○ 16-20 years
- ○ 21-25 years
- ○ 26 years or more

9) What national certification(s) do you hold? Check all that apply.
- ❑ CSC
- ❑ CI and CT
- ❑ NAD Level IV
- ❑ NAD Level V
- ❑ NIC (certified)
- ❑ NIC Advanced
- ❑ NIC Master
- ❑ SC:L
- ❑ OTC or OIC:C
- ❑ EIPA (4.0 or higher)
- ❑ Other [   ]

10) Did you graduate from an interpreting program? [If "No," proceed to quesiton 13.]
- ○ Yes
- ○ No

11) If you graduated from an interpreting program, what type of program was it?
- ○ Associate's degree
- ○ Bachelor's degree
- ○ Master's degree
- ○ Certificate
- ○ Diploma
- ○ Other [   ]

12) If you graduated from an interpreting program, what year did you graduate from the interpreting program?

[   ]

13) Indicate your primary type of employment as an interpreter.
- ○ Staff
- ○ Freelance
- ○ I do not currently work as an interpreter
- ○ Other [   ]

14) Approximately what percentage of your interpreting work involves working as a team?
- ○ 0-10%
- ○ 11-20%
- ○ 21-30%
- ○ 31-40%
- ○ 41-50%
- ○ 51-60%
- ○ 61-70%
- ○ 71-80%
- ○ 81-90%
- ○ 91-100%

15) Check all of the following that apply.
- ❑ I have never had training in team interpreting
- ❑ I have had training in team interpreting
- ❑ I have taught team interpreting (as a workshop or class)
- ❑ I am an interpreter educator or an interpreter workshop presenter

QUESTIONS ON TEAM INTERPRETING

For all of the following, please make your comments as concise and clear as possible. You may write a short list or a short paragraph to answer each question.

16) Define 'team interpreting' in your own words.

[   ]

17) What makes for an effective interpreting team (of two hearing interpreters)?

18) Describe the characteristics of an interpreter that you would prefer to work with.

19) What should teams discuss–or at least have mutual agreement/understanding about–before teaming together?

20) What are some specific ways that a 'feed' interpreter can support the 'on' interpreter during an interpretation?

21) What are some specific ways that interpreters can support each other during an interpretation–other than by 'feeding'?

22) Teams may function differently (work with each other differently) depending on the interpreters and the particular context. Please give an example or two of how teams may function differently. (optional)

MODALITY AND LANGUAGE

The following three questions relate to the modality and language that are used by interpreters to communicate with each other during the interpretation.

23) What modality do you tend to use?
- ○ Spoken
- ○ Signed
- ○ Written
- ○ other

24) What language do you tend to use?
- ○ English
- ○ ASL
- ○ nonverbal communicaiton
- ○ other

25) Explain why you tend to use the above modality and language.

[ ]

OTHER COMMENTS (OPTIONAL)

26) Please write here anything else you want to say about team interpreting that was not covered above. (optional)

[ ]

Submit Completed Survey

APPENDIX III

APPENDIX III. DATA ON THE SURVEY PARTICIPANTS

Appendix III supplies the reader with specific demographic information and other data about the respondents to the survey on team interpreting. This Appendix makes use of tables and charts, as well as summarizing paragraphs, to report on this detailed information.

Forty-three respondents (93.5%) are female and three (6.5%) are male. In terms of the ancestry of the respondents (race and ethnicity), forty-two (91.3%) of the respondents reported having European ancestry, two (4.3%) reported having Asian or Pacific Islander ancestry, one (2.2%) reported having African ancestry, one (2.2%) reported having Hispanic/ Latino ancestry (this person also reported having European ancestry), and one person (2.2%) did not identify an ancestry. See Table 1.

Ancestry	*Number*	*Percentage*
European	42	91.3%
Asian or Pacific Islander	2	4.3%
African	1	2.2%
Hispanic/Latino	1	2.2%[1]
Unidentified	1	2.2%

Table 1. Ancestry (Race/Ethnicity) of respondents

Respondents ranged from 23 to 59 years of age, with an average age of 44.5 years and a mode (the most frequently reported age) of 44 years. See Table 2 (the numbers in bold lettering indicate responses of four or more).

Age	Number	Percentage
23	1	2.2%
25	1	2.2%
26	1	2.2%
29	1	2.2%
32	1	2.2%
33	1	2.2%
36	2	4.3%
38	1	2.2%
41	1	2.2%
43	**4**	**8.7%**
44	**5**	**10.9%**
45	1	2.2%
46	2	4.3%
47	**4**	**8.7%**
48	2	4.3%
49	1	2.2%
50	2	4.3%
51	**4**	**8.7%**
52	2	4.3%
53	2	4.3%
54	2	4.3%
55	1	2.2%
56	1	2.2%
57	1	2.2%
58	1	2.2%
59	1	2.2%

Table 2. Age of respondents

Forty-five of the forty-six respondents (97.8%) reported that they were hearing, and one person (2.2%) reported being hard of hearing. Of the forty-six respondents, eight (17.4%) reported that they were codas (children of Deaf adults) and one respondent (2.2%) reported having other Deaf relatives.

The respondents represent all of the regions of the Registry of Interpreters for the Deaf (RID), as shown in Figure 1. A total of seven interpreters (15.2%) responded from each of the following three Regions: I (the Northeast), III (the Upper Midwest), and IV (the Central West & Western Midwest). The most responses were from Region V (the West; eleven responses; 23.9%), and the second most were from Region II (the Southeast; nine responses; 19.6%). It was not possible to identify the state of residency of five respondents (10.9%). Either these five respondents did not use the drop-down menu to select a state, or their selection had timed out and the selection returned to the default, so their state of origin could not be determined.

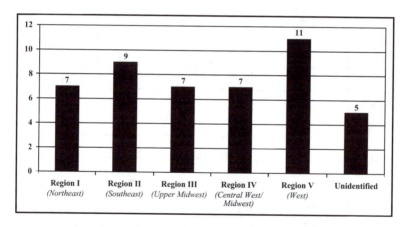

Figure 1. The RID regions of respondents

The respondents to the survey comprise a highly experienced group of interpreters overall, with the vast majority of them (80.4%) having over ten years of interpreting experience. In fact, slightly over two-thirds of the respondents (67.4%) had sixteen or more years of interpreting experience. See Table 3 (note the high percentages for the years appearing in bold type). In contrast, only nine respondents (19.6%) reported that they had ten years of experience or less. The average years of experience is 20.5 years (which is both the mean and the median). The mode, however, is twenty-six or more years of interpreting experience.

1-5 years	6	13%
6-10 years	3	6.5%
11-15 years	6	13%
16-20 years	**8**	**17.4%**
21-25 years	**8**	**17.4%**
26+ years	**15**	**32.6%**
TOTAL	*46*	*100%*

Table 3. The respondents' number of years of interpreting experience

The certifications held by these nationally certified interpreters appear in Figure 2. Thirty-three of the forty-six respondents (71.7%) held the CI and CT. Seventeen of these interpreters with the CI and CT (52%) held only the CI and CT, and sixteen of these interpreters who held the CI/CT (48%) also held at least one other certification. The majority of the interpreters who responded to the survey held more than one certification. See Figure 2 for the certifications held and Figure 3 for the number of multiple certifications held.[2]

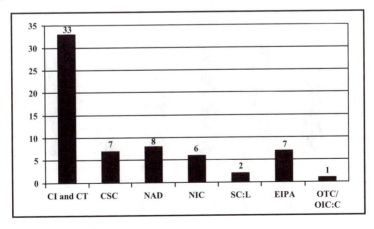

Figure 2. Certifications of respondents

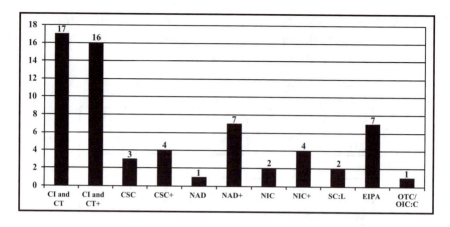

Figure 3. Multiple certifications held by respondents

Figure 4 indicates the number of years these respondents have been certified. In addition to having many years of interpreting experience and holding multiple certifications, the respondents also have held their certifications for many years, on average. Twenty-nine of the interpreters (63%) had been certified for eleven or more years and seventeen (37%) had been certified for ten years or less. Most interpreters, then, have worked as interpreters longer than they have been certified (compare Table 3 and Figure 4).

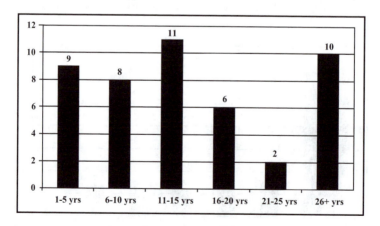

Figure 4. Number of years certified

This group of respondents was also highly educated. Over two-thirds of the respondents (thirty-two of the forty-six respondents; 69.6%) held at least a Bachelor's degree, and twenty-two of the forty-six respondents (47.8%) have taken coursework beyond a baccalaureate or have completed graduate studies.[3] See Figure 5. Of those who did not hold at least a Bachelor's degree, eight (17.4%) held an Associate's degree; five (10.9%) had a high school diploma or GED; and one (2.2%) had taken some college coursework, but did not hold a college degree. The educational backgrounds of the group can be summarized as follows: (1) a little under one-third (fourteen of the forty-six respondents; 30.4%) held an Associate's degree or high school diploma (or equivalent), and (2) the majority--thirty-two; 69.6%--held at least a Bachelor's degree, and of those, a large number (eighteen of the forty-six respondents; 39.1%) held a Master's degree or higher.

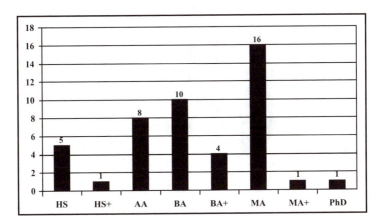

Figure 5. Educational background of respondents

A survey question also asked if respondents had graduated from an interpreter preparation program. A slight majority–twenty-five (54.3%)–of respondents did not graduate from an interpreting program. See Figure 6. Of the twenty-one respondents (45.7%) who graduated from an interpreting program, thirteen of these twenty-one respondents (61.9%) graduated from a certificate program, five of the twenty-one (23.8%) graduated from a baccalaureate degree program, and three (14.3%) graduated from an associate's degree program.[4] See Figure 7.

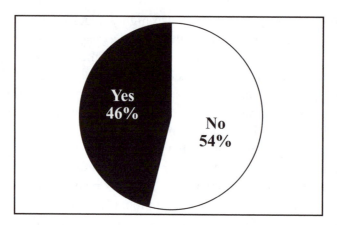

Figure 6. Interpreting Program Graduates

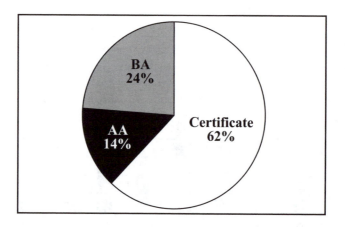

Figure 7. Type of Interpreting Program/Degree

The survey also asked what percentage of the interpreters' work involves team interpreting. Almost four-fifths of the respondents (thirty-six of the forty-six responses; 78.3%) reported that 50% or less of their interpreting work involved teaming, and 41-50% was the mode (with nine respondents selecting 41-50%; 19.6%). Only ten respondents (21.7%) stated that over 50% of their work involves teaming. The average percentage of team interpreting work reported is 31.3%. See Figure 8.

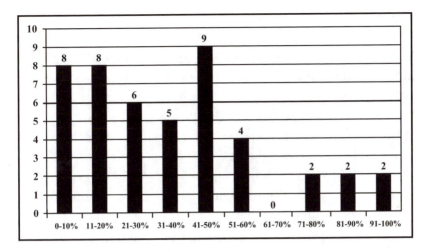

Figure 8. Percentage of Interpreting Work that Involves Teaming

It is not possible from the survey to determine if there is a greater tendency for freelance interpreters or staff interpreters to be involved in team interpreting. However, the responses of three specific staff interpreters may indicate that two particular groups of interpreters may team interpret the least. Two interpreters who work for a video relay service (VRS) reported that 0-10% of their interpreting work involved teaming and one interpreter reported working in an educational system (high school level).[v] Although this is a small number, it may be telling, as most interpreters would not be surprised that these two types of positions make use of team interpreting the least. However, more research is needed to further determine what kinds of positions (certain types of staff positions, certain freelance assignments, etc.) may utilize team interpreting more often than others. The fact that respondents report that 31.3% of assignments (on average) are team interpreted indicates the prevalence of team interpreting in the field.

ENDNOTES

[1] As mentioned above, one person reported having both Hispanic/Latino ancestry and European ancestry. This person's response is counted here in both of those categories.

[2] Some respondents also reported that they held the following certifications: IC (4), TC (4), RSC (1). The number in parentheses is the number of respondents holding each certification, with some respondents holding more than one of these certifications.

[3] Stauffer, et al., 1999, also report a large majority of interpreters have a baccalaureate degree or higher.

[4] Two of the interpreters, who graduated from a certificate program in the 1980s, reported that their programs were less than two months long.

[5] One of these interpreters who was employed by VRS worked full-time for VRS, and the other interpreter worked part-time for VRS and part-time on a freelance basis.

REFERENCES

*AIIC (Association Internationale des Interprètes de Conférence
[International Association of Conference Interpreters]) research
unit report.* (2002, February). Retrieved from http://www.aiic.net/.../
ViewAttachment.cfm/a467p657-897.pdf?&filename=a467p657-897.
pdf&page_id=657.

American heritage dictionary (4th ed.). (2001). New York: Dell.

Angelelli, C. (2003). The visible co-participant: The interpreter's role
in doctor-patient encounters. In M. Metzger, S. Collins, V. Dively, &
R. Shaw (Eds.), *From topic boundaries to omission: New research on
interpretation* (pp. 3-26). Washington, DC: Gallaudet University
Press.

Baker-Shenk, C. (1992). The interpreter: Machine, advocate, or ally?
In J. Plant-Moeller (Ed.), *Expanding Horizons* (pp. 119-140). Silver
Spring, MD: RID Publications.

Baker-Shenk, C., & Cokely, D. (1980). *American Sign Language:
A teacher's resource text on grammar and culture.* Silver Spring, MD:
TJ Publishers.

Berk-Seligson, S. (1990). *The bilingual courtroom: Court interpreters in
the judicial process.* Chicago, IL: University of Chicago Press.

Bienvenu, MJ. (1989). Process diagnostics: The Deaf perspective. In
S. Wilcox (Ed.), *New Dimensions in Interpreter Education:
Evaluation and Critique* (pp. 99-112). Conference of Interpreter
Trainers.

Birr, R. (2008, January). Team interpreting: Giving and receiving
feedback. *VIEWS*, 8-9.

Carnet, G. (2006, November/December). Team interpreting: Does
it really work? [Featured article]. *American Translators Association
Chronicle.* Retrieved from http://www.atanet.org/chronicle/feature_
article_nov_dec2006.php

Cassell, J. (Producer). (2006a). *Viewpoints: Deaf education.* [DVD]. Eden Prairie, MN: Sign Enhancers. Available from http://www. signenhancers.com

Cassell, J. (Producer). (2006b). *Viewpoints: Deaf culture.* [DVD]. Eden Prairie, MN: Sign Enhancers. Available from http://www. signenhancers.com

Cerney, B. (2005). *The interpreting handbook, Part 1.* Colorado Springs, CO: Hand & Mind Publishing.

Chafin Seal, B. (2004). *Best practices in educational interpreting (2nd ed.).* Needham Heights, MA: Allyn & Bacon.

Cogen, C., Forestal, E., Hills, R., & Hollrah, B. (Writers/directors). (2006). *Deaf interpreting: Team strategies.* [DVD]. Washington, D.C.: Gallaudet University Academic Technology TV & Media Production Services, Graduate School and Professional Programs.

Cohen-Gilbert, H., & D'Entremont, L. (Producers). (2007). *Effective team interpreting.* [DVD]. McKinney, TX: Hand in Hand.

Cokely, D. (1992). *Interpretation: A sociolinguistic model.* Burtonsville, MD: Linstok Press, Inc.

Cokely, D. (2001). Interpreting culturally rich realities: Research implications for successful interpretations. *Journal of Interpretation*, 1-45.

Cokely, D., & Hawkins, J. (2003). Interpreting in teams: A pilot study on requesting and offering support. *Journal of Interpretation*, 49-93.

Colonomos, B. (1992). *The interpreting process.* Unpublished manuscript.

Colonomos, B. (1995). *Depth of processing.* Unpublished manuscript.

Colonomos, B. (1996). *Pedagogical model of the interpreting process.* Unpublished manuscript.

Colonomos, B. (Producer). (2001). *Community module: Group discussion and analysis.* [DVD]. Burtonsville, MD: Sign Media, Inc. Available from http://www.signmedia.com.

Covey, S. (2004). *The 7 habits of highly effective people.* New York, NY: Free Press.

Dean, R., & Pollard, R. (2001). Application of demand-control theory to sign language interpreting: Implications for stress and interpreter training. *Journal of Deaf Studies and Deaf Education, 6*(1), 1-14.

Festinger, N. (1999, Summer/Fall). When is a team not a team? *Proteus: Newsletter of the National Association of Judiciary Interpreters and Translators (NAJIT), 8*(3-4). Retrieved from http://www.najit.org/members_only/proteus/v8n3-4/festinger_v8n3-4.htm

Fisher, T. (1993). Team interpreting: The team approach. *Journal of Interpretation,* 167-173.

Frishberg. N. (1990). *Interpreting: An introduction (Revised ed.).* Silver Spring, MD: RID Publications.

Gish, S. (1987). "I understood all the words, but I missed the point": A goal-to-detail/detail-to-goal strategy for text analysis. In M. McIntire (Ed.), *Proceedings of the Sixth National Convention: New Dimensions in Interpreter Education: Curriculum and Instruction* (pp. 125-137). RID Publications.

Gish, S. (1993). A Vygotskian perspective on interpreter assessment. In E. Winston (Ed.), *Student Competencies: Defining, Teaching, and Evaluating* (pp. 19-44). Conference of Interpreter Trainers.

Gordon, P., & Magler, M. (2007). *The mentor's companion: A practical guide to mentoring.* Alexandria, VA: RID Press.

Gross, D. (2009, Winter). Overuse pain: An unavoidable professional liability? *VIEWS*, 24-25.

Gross, D. (2010, Winter). Managing predisposing factors to injury. *VIEWS*, 21-22.

Halliday, M.A.K. (1978). *Language as a social semiotic: The social interpretation of language and meaning.* Baltimore, MD: Edward Arnold, Ltd.

Hatrak, M., Craft, D., Cundy, L., & Vincent, S. (2007, December). Who comes first: The Deaf presenter or the interpreter? *VIEWS,* 12-14.

Hauser, P., Finch, K., & Hauser, A. (Eds.) (2008). *Deaf professionals and designated interpreters: A new paradigm.* Washington, DC: Gallaudet University Press.

Hoza, J. (1999). Saving face: The interpreter and politeness. *Journal of Interpretation*, 39-68.

Hoza, J. (2003). Toward an interpreter sensibility: Three levels of ethical analysis and a comprehensive model of ethical decision-making for interpreters. *Journal of Interpretation*, 1-48.

Hoza, J. (2007a). *It's not what you sign, it's how you sign it: Politeness in American Sign Language.* Washington, DC: Gallaudet University Press.

Hoza, J. (2007b). How interpreters convey social meaning: Implications for interpreted interaction. *Journal of Interpretation*, 39-68.

Humphrey, J., & Alcorn, B. (2007). *So you want to be an interpreter? An introduction to sign language interpreting (4th ed.).* Seattle, WA: H & H Publishing Company.

Jones, A. (2007). Team interpreting: The good teammate. *In Innovative Practices in Team Interpreting: 14th EFSLI AGM & Conference* (pp. 36-39). Prague, Czech Republic: European Forum of Sign Language Interpreters.

Joos, M. (1968). *The five clocks.* New York, NY: Harcourt Brace & World, Inc.

Kanda, J. (1992). Demographic profile and brain dominance preferences among certified sign language interpreters: Implications for educators. In L. Swabey (Ed.), *The Challenge of the 90's: New Standards in Interpreter Education, Proceedings of the Eighth National Convention* (pp. 23-49). Conference of Interpreter Trainers.

Kannapell, B. (1993). *Language choice—identity choice.* Burtonsville, MD: Linstok Press.

Kinsella, T. (1997). Beyond correction and critique: Working in teams. *Journal of Interpretation.* 115-119.

Ladd, P. (2003). *Understanding Deaf culture: In search of Deafhood.* Tonawanda, NY: Multilingual Matters, Ltd.

Lane, H., Hoffmeister, R., & Bahan, B. (1996). *A journey into the Deaf-World.* San Diego, CA: DawnSignPress.

Larson, M. (1998). *Meaning-based translation: A guide to cross-language equivalence (2nd Ed.).* Mildred L. Larson. Lanham, MD: University Press of America.

Lucas, C., & Valli, C. (1992). *Language contact in the American Deaf community.* San Diego, CA: Academic Press.

Metzger, M. (1999). *Sign language interpreting: Deconstructing the myth of neutrality.* Washington, DC: Gallaudet University Press.

Mindess, A. (2006). *Reading between the signs: Intercultural communication for sign language interpreters (2nd ed.).* Boston, MA: Intercultural Press.

Mitchell, R., & Karchmer, M. (2004). Chasing the mythical 10%: Parental hearing status of deaf and hard of hearing students in the United States. *Sign Language Studies, 4*(2), 138-163.

Moore, M., and Levitan, L. (2003). *For hearing people only: Answers to some of the most commonly asked questions about the Deaf community, its culture, and the "Deaf reality" (3rd ed.).* Rochester, NY: Deaf Life Press.

Moser-Mercer, B., Kunzli, A., & Korac, M. (1998). Prolonged turns in interpreting: Effects on quality, physiological, and psychological stress (Pilot study). *Interpreting, 3*(1), 47-64.

NAD-RID code of professional conduct. (2005). Retrieved from http://www.rid.org

NAJIT (National Association of Judiciary Interpreters and Translators) position paper: Team interpreting in the courtroom. (2007). Retrieved from http://www.najit.org/Documents/Team%20Interpreting_052007.pdf

Napier, J., Carmichael, A., & Wiltshire, A. (2008). Look-pause-nod: A linguistic case study of a Deaf professional and interpreters working together. In P. Hauser, K. Finch, & A. Hauser (Eds.), *Deaf professionals and designated interpreters: A new paradigm* (pp. 22-42). Washington, DC: Gallaudet University Press.

Neidle, C., Kegl, J., MacLaughlin, D., Bahan, B., & Lee, R. G. (2000). *The syntax of American Sign Language: Functional categories and hierarchical structure.* Cambridge, MA: MIT Press.

Nettles, C. (2010, Winter). What have we done for you lately? The RID annual report to the members. *VIEWS*, 49-71.

Neumann Solow, S. (1981). *Sign language interpreting: A basic resource book.* Silver Spring, MD: National Association of the Deaf.

Norris, R. (1996). Repetitive strain injuries (RSI) in sign language interpreters: Evaluation, treatment and prevention. *VIEWS, 13*(1), 1 & 30-31.

Padden, C., & Humphries, T. (1988). *Deaf in America: Voices from a culture.* Cambridge, MA: Harvard University Press.

Padden, C., & Humphries, T. (2005). *Inside Deaf culture.* Cambridge, MA: Harvard University Press.

Plant-Moeller, J. (1991). Team interpreting. In J. Plant-Moeller (Ed.), *Expanding Horizons: Proceedings of the Twelfth National RID Convention* (pp. 156-165). Silver Spring, MD: RID Publications.

Pollard, R., & Dean, R. (Eds.). (2008). *Applications of Demand Control Schema in Interpreter Education: Proceedings of the RID Pre-Conference Meeting, August 3, 2007.* Rochester, NY: University of Rochester.

Richards, T. (2008). *Establishing a freelance interpretation business: Professional guidance for sign language interpreters (3rd ed.).* Hillsboro, OR: Butte Publications, Inc.

RID (Registry of Interpreters for the Deaf) standard practice paper: Team interpreting. (2007). Retrieved from http://www.rid.org/ UserFiles/File/pdfs/117.pdf

Roush, D. (2007). Indirect strategies in American Sign Language requests and refusals: Deconstructing the Deaf-as-direct stereotype. In M. Metzger & E. Fleetwood (Eds.), *Translation, sciolinguistic, and consumer issues in interpreting* (pp. 103-156). Washington, DC: Gallaudet University Press.

Roy, C. (2000a). *Interpreting as a discourse process.* New York, NY: Oxford University Press.

Roy, C. (Ed.). (2000b). *Innovative practices for teaching sign language interpreters.* Washington, DC: Gallaudet University Press.

Sanderson, G. (1987). Overuse syndrome among sign language interpreters. *Journal of Interpretation*, 73-78.

Seleskovitch, D. (1978). *Interpreting for international conferences: Problems of language and communication.* Washington, DC: Pen & Booth.

Seleskovitch, D. (1994). *Interpreting for international conferences: Problems of language and communication (2nd ed.).* Washington, DC: Pen & Booth.

Shaw, R. (1989). Process diagnostics: A powerful tool. In S. Wilcox (Ed.), *New Dimensions in Interpreter Education: Evaluation and Critique* (pp. 143-152). Conference of Interpreter Trainers.

Shaw, R. (1995). Practicing our standards: Improving working conditions benefits interpreters and consumers. *VIEWS, 12*(2), 2 & 19.

Sluis, J., & De Wit, M. (2007). Getting the most out of it: Developing the individual and the team. In *Innovative Practices in Team Interpreting: 14th EFSLI AGM & Conference* (pp. 12-14). Prague, Czech Republic: European Forum of Sign Language Interpreters.

Stauffer, L., Burch, D., & Boone, S. (1999). A study of the demographics of attendees at the 1997 biennial convention of the Registry of Interpreters for the Deaf, Inc. *Journal of Interpretation*, 105-116.

Stewart, D., Schein, J., & Cartwright, B. E. (1998). *Sign language interpreting: Exploring its art and science.* Needham Heights, MA: Allyn & Bacon.

Vidal, M. (1997, Winter). New study on fatigue confirms need for working in teams. *Proteus, 6*(1). Retrieved from http://www.najit.org/proteus/back_issues/vidal2.htm

Wadensjö, C. (1998). *Interpreting as interaction*. New York, NY: Addison Wesley Longman.

Walker, B. (1994). Teaming. *VIEWS*, 3, 21, 22.

Walker, J. (2007). Co-working to co-interpreting: Definition, application, and curriculum. In *Innovative Practices in Team Interpreting: 14th EFSLI AGM & Conference* (pp. 40-44). Prague, Czech Republic: European Forum of Sign Language Interpreters.

Wilcox, S. (Ed.). (1989). *American Deaf culture: An anthology.* Burtonsville, MD: Linstok Press.

Winston, E., & Monikowski, C. (2000). Discourse mapping: Developing textual coherence skills in interpreters. In C. Roy (Ed.), *Innovative practices for teaching sign language interpreters* (pp. 15-66). Washington, DC: Gallaudet University Press.

Witter-Merithew, A. (1986, October). Claiming our destiny. *VIEWS*, 12.

Woodward, J. (1982). *How you gonna get to heaven if you can't talk with Jesus: On depathologizing deafness.* Silver Spring, MD: TJ.

Yates, L. (2008, January). Team interpreting in a religious setting. *VIEWS*, 1 & 15.